Vow of Love

Living an extraordinary life of compassion

Jetsunma Ahkön Norbu Lhamo

Wild Dakini LLC
P.O. Box 304
Poolesville, Maryland 20837 USA
www.wilddakini.com

First edition, revised

Printed in USA.

ISBN 978-0-9855245-1-7
Ebook ISBN 978-0-9855245-4-8
1. Spirituality 2. Buddhism

Library of Congress Control Number 2017915862

Vow of Love: Living an Extraordinary Life of Compassion by Jetsunma Ahkön Norbu Lhamo

Cover photo by Ted Kurkowski depicts the top of the Migyur Dorje Stupa at Kunzang Palyul Chöling in Poolesville Maryland, USA.

Cover and book design by Ani Atara Heiss.

I dedicate this book first and foremost to the memory of His Holiness, the sublime Third Drubwang Pema Norbu Rinpoche; the eleventh Throne holder of the Palyul Lineage. I also dedicate this book to his heart sons, the extraordinary twelfth Throne holder of the Palyul Lineage, His Holiness Karma Kuchen Rinpoche, His Eminence Khentul Gyangkhang Rinpoche and His Eminence Mugsang Kuchen Rinpoche.

CONTENTS

FOREWORD

On June 17, 1985 a line of black limousines appeared at Dulles Airport. A large Chinese delegation held white scarves and flowers. Flash bulbs exploded.

The sea of black-clad Chinese parted, and a short, stocky Tibetan monk emerged. He walked right past the Chinese . . . and directly toward a young woman, who burst into tears.

Catharine Burroughs didn't know that this man was venerated as a "Living Buddha," that devotees sometimes scooped up the earth where he had stepped. She was there because he had requested an opportunity to thank her for helping to raise money for young Tibetan monks.

Soon His Holiness Penor Rinpoche and his entourage were picnicking in Catharine's backyard with the students of her spiritual group. Her students were amazed when Penor Rinpoche declared, with delighted amusement, that Catharine had been teaching them Buddhism.

Against a background of New Age spiritual groups, Catharine offered something very different. Her students were inspired by her radiant, unconditional compassion. As they sensed it in her, they also sensed—by some sort of spiritual osmosis—the possibility of this compassion within them. They too could learn to love all beings. They could embrace them with kindness and compassion, and this was a rational thing to do.

After connecting with Catharine, her students were no longer comfortable inhabiting a "me-centered" world. She gave them what she called "the courage necessary to break that habitual tendency of self-concern—the deadness of living like that." She asked them to "come forth into a world that needs you."

It was this teacher that Penor Rinpoche recognized as Jetsunma Ahkön Lhamo, the reincarnation of a seventeenth century yogini.

Jetsunma's teachings convey complex aspects of Tibetan Buddhism to modern Western audiences in simple words. Her delivery is lively, graphic, and earthy.

Jetsunma has said that before teaching, she asks in prayer to be of benefit to the audience she will soon address. And strangely enough, after she speaks, many are gratefully left with the bewildering impression that she is speaking to them alone, saying precisely that which is currently, vitally helpful. The appropriateness of her words often seems uncanny.

Again and again, Jetsunma returns in her teachings to the fundamental need for compassion: "To me, compassion is not a feeling at all. It is not an emotion. It is logical. It is meaningful. I find no other excuse for living." Without it she would feel lost, she has said, "Like a bee buzzing around in a jar. Whether or not people are Buddhist, she insists, they have a job to do, "and that job is to develop a fervent, sincere aspiration to be of true benefit to others."

— Eleanor and Woody Rowe

ACKNOWLEDGEMENTS

Many people helped bring this book to completion. We are grateful to all of them.

We thank Eleanor and Woody Rowe, long time students of Jetsunma's, for their eloquence in the Foreword, capturing Jetsunma's intention to go beyond Buddhist concepts to call forth the compassion that is innate in all of us.

Thanks to Ani Kunzang Drolma who organized and edited this series of Jetsunma's teachings; and to Michael Brunk for his attention to detail in the final edit. Ani Aileen Williams provided the cover photo from the Kunzang Palyul Chöling Archives and Ted Kurkowski took the photograph. Ani Atara Heiss designed the cover and the layout of the book. We also appreciate the contributions of Ani Megan Gilana, Ani Alyce Louise and Rodrigo Vacaflor.

We take full responsibility for any errors or mistakes that were made in the course of preparing this book.

May this book be of benefit.

Ani Rinchen Khandro and Ani Tenzin Wangmo
Wild Dakini Publication Co-ordinators

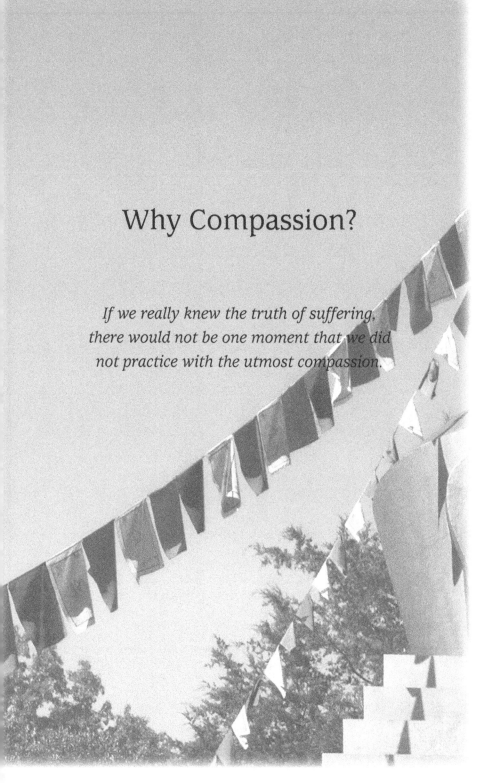

Why Compassion?

If we really knew the truth of suffering, there would not be one moment that we did not practice with the utmost compassion.

I would like to talk about a subject that is of the utmost importance to everyone. The subject is compassion.

You may think, "Oh, I know all about compassion. I've been a Dharma practitioner for a long time. I've had many teachings about compassion." Or you might think, "I'm a person with a good heart. I try not to do any harm, and I try to help people. Therefore, I know about compassion." If we hold these ideas in our heart, we have already lost precious opportunities, and will continue to lose more, because the cultivation of compassion in the heart and mind is an ongoing process.

Even if you come into this world with a compassionate ideal you must still cultivate the idea of compassion as though it were the first time you ever thought of it. Due to intense spiritual practice in the past, you may have been born into this lifetime with the idea that you want to be of benefit to sentient beings. Yet still you must cultivate the idea of compassion everyday, as though it were a delicate orchid that could die in an unnatural environment. Until we are supremely enlightened, we have obscurations of our mind that will fight against the idea of compassion.

There is no one on this earth, unless they are supremely realized, who has the purified mind of compassion. If you have been meditating for many years, and think compassion is a baby subject and you're far beyond that, or if you think because you've practiced for a long time, compassion is just one of the beginner studies, and now you'd like to get on to the mystical or the "higher" Dzogchen teachings, then I think you're making a mistake. I hope that you will relax your mind and come to the point where you commit to studying compassion deeply and profoundly, as though it were your mother. You should have that kind of intimate relationship with the idea of compassion. You should seek to be taught by it. You should seek to be suckled by the mind of compassion. You should seek to be nourished in that way.

In a superficial way the idea of compassion can seem very simple, and we might make the mistake of thinking that we understand it. But if we study compassion deeply, eventually we will come to understand that the ultimate view of compassion is enlightenment itself. It is the natural, primordial wisdom state itself. That's why compassion isn't truly known until we reach supreme enlightenment.

Compassion is the foundation of the Buddhist path. Without it, like any house that does not have a firm foundation, the house will crumble. It will not stand. One's motivation to practice must be compassion. If your motivation is not compassion, it will be very difficult to firmly stick to the commitment to practice and meditate every day. I feel for those who say, "I'd really like to practice. I would really like to have a time in my life everyday to meditate, and yet I don't have the discipline. I don't have the strength. I don't have the commitment." If you have the right motivation, if you want to do this solely and purely from the point of view of compassion, you will find the time and you will find the commitment and you will find a way to do it. For those who have tried to meditate everyday or be consistent in their practice, if they can't do it, my feeling is somehow the foundation of compassion isn't strong enough.

If we could make the idea of compassion so strong that it becomes a burning fire consuming our hearts, until we are nothing but a flame. If the need to benefit others becomes so strong that it's irresistible. If the understanding that others are suffering so unbearably in realms that we cannot even see, let alone the realms we can, that we cannot rest until we find a way to be of some lasting benefit to them. If these things can truly become part of our minds, we will find the strength to practice.

How do you find the strength to breathe? "Well," you say, "that's easy. Breathing is a reflex. I have to breathe. If I don't breathe, I die." What if you could cultivate the understanding that all sentient beings are filled with suffering that is inconceivable in its magnitude and that there are non-physical realms of existence we are not even aware of, filled with suffering? What if you could cultivate this understanding so deeply that, because of your realization, compassion and profound generosity became as much a reflex as breathing? That is possible.

"Well," you say, "I don't have that kind of understanding. I'm just not like that. I can't make myself really buy into that." Let me comfort you with this awareness. Unless you are supremely enlightened you are not born with that perfect understanding. No one is. No one is born with enough understanding of the suffering of others, and an affinity with the idea of compassion, to create that perfect discipline naturally. That understanding comes only through its cultivation, and we must cultivate that understanding consistently every day.

If you've never practiced the Buddhadharma before, or if you're interested in practicing, or if you have practiced some general meditation and you feel it's time to move on to a path that is more stable or well known, then you're in a perfect place for this teaching. You can start practicing one of the most important teachings of the Buddha right now. You can begin to cultivate the mind of compassion. How might you do this? First of all, you might look around and examine physical existence.

In America, we hide our suffering. We have very little knowledge of real suffering, and I think that's one reason why it's very difficult for Westerners to practice a pure and disciplined path. We think we understand suffering because we have experienced loneliness, or because when we were kids we had the measles, or because we have gone through marriages and divorces. Or maybe we've seen some sickness or poverty. For these reasons, we think we understand suffering, and we do to some extent. These are valid sufferings.

But there's a funny thing about our culture that we must understand. We are actually hidden from the sufferings of our culture. When people are deformed, handicapped, mentally or terminally ill, they are taken away from the mainstream of society and they are hidden. Or if we are considered unpresentable to most people, we have plastic surgery or we have some kind of therapy that makes us like everyone else. In fact, if we examine the healing process in American medicine, part of that process is to become like other people. We are made to look like other people.

In other countries around the world suffering is more evident, for many different reasons: those countries may not be as technologically advanced as our country, or their culture may be an older society in which suffering has become more the norm and it is not such a shock to see it. Or perhaps poverty is a factor.

I will describe how I felt when I first went to India. I couldn't bear it. I don't claim to be so compassionate; I too have to cultivate the idea of compassion every day. But I remember seeing people walking the streets with arms and legs missing, eaten up by leprosy. I saw mothers and fathers maim their children, not because they hated them or because they were cruel to them, but because that would give them a deformity they could use for begging. That would be the only way they could ensure their survival. There was no other way for them to get food. What do we do for our children? We might send ours to school. In the streets of India, they have to prepare them in a different way.

Suffering is a part of the fabric of the society in India, and it's very evident. I remember walking down the street in Delhi. There was a young boy who must have been twelve; it was hard to tell, he was so small. He was lying on a rag, a tattered blanket, and he was dying. He was so thin that he looked like the pictures of starvation we see from Ethiopia. He was beyond thin. His bones were sticking out, his belly swollen, his tongue hanging out. And next to him were a few coins and a candy bar. Someone had thrown them down for him.

We don't see that in our culture. We don't understand it. We think that the things we've gone through—the divorces, not being able to pay the light bill, the heartbreak of psoriasis, the things we consider so awesome—are the real sufferings of the world. But they are not all the world has to endure. Look at the animal realm. We know what our animals are like. They get fed everyday and they have it pretty good. But not all animals are like them. If we go to different countries, we see beasts of burden that are treated in horrible ways. We see animals that are denied their natural environment.

Humans and animals are only two life forms. According to the Buddha's teachings, there are many different life forms, many of which are non-physical. How we appear, how we manifest, what form we take has to do with the qualities of our mind. If we are filled with hate, we are reborn in a hell realm. Why is that so hard to understand? When you are filled with hate now, even as a human being, aren't you in your own private hell? Have you ever gone through a period where you were so filled with anger that everything you saw became ugly and you managed to distort it somehow? Each of us has lived in a private hell. Why is it so hard to believe that we are capable of living in or creating a situation like that? If your mind is capable of having a nightmare, then rebirth in a hell realm is a possibility.

Have you ever been needy? Have you ever gone through a period in your life when you needed approval, or love, or some kind of nourishment so badly, that you were in a state of despair? When people did reach out to you, they couldn't get through? Each of us, for at least one moment in our lives, has experienced this. Why then is it so hard to understand that these kinds of existences really do exist?

Having understood that this is logical, having examined your own mind truthfully—and truthfully is the key—and found the residue of these experiences in your mind, you can allow yourself to go more deeply into the recognition that the Buddha was right. There is suffering in cyclic existence.

We have to think also of our own suffering. We must think that even if we have a TV, a car, a house, and all of the things that we are taught to desire, there will be a point at which we cannot take them with us. There will be a point at which they will do us no good. That point, of course, is death. All of the efforts that we've gone through to get those things will have been wasted.

Long-time Dharma practitioners may think, "I really wish she'd get on with it. I know this." I have to tell you, if you really knew the truth of suffering, there would not be one moment that you did not practice with the utmost compassion. There would not be one moment when you thought only of yourself and your needs, and of the temporary gratifications you think you must have. Yet you still have many of those moments.

You may ask, "Why do I have to think about suffering? Why is it that the Buddha talks about suffering and nobody else does? Why is it that today's New Age thinkers are saying, 'I want to be me. I want to be free,' and the Buddha is still talking about suffering after thousands and thousands of years?" It is because the Buddha has a teaching that is very logical and very real.

If we want to exit a room, but there is a chair between us and the door, we have a number of choices. We can say that the chair is not there. We can pretend that the chair is not an obstacle to our passing through the room and that it's not important. Or we can notice that the chair is there and get on with our journey by walking around it. That is the essence of the Buddha's teaching. The Buddha doesn't stop at saying, "There is suffering." The Buddha follows that by saying, "There is a way out of suffering." And that's the ticket. You cannot motivate yourself to follow the path out of suffering until you generate the commitment through the realization of suffering. You can't make yourself walk around the chair to get to the door until you face the fact that the chair is blocking your way. You have to look at the chair.

It isn't only about walking around a chair so that you can get to the other side of the room, so that you can get out the door. There's more to it than that. You must understand that your commitment is two-fold. In order to become the deepened practitioner that you must be, to really sink your teeth into the Buddhadharma, you must have compassion for others that is so strong and so extraordinary it will nourish you even when you are dry.

There are many Dharma practitioners who practice for many years, go on retreat, and even take ordination. Then at some point, some karmic switch flips in their minds and suddenly they're finished with Dharma! They don't want to do Dharma anymore. They're on to something else. We may think that's strange, but it has happened, especially to Westerners. It's not uncommon for a Westerner to practice Dharma sincerely and then flip tracks, and go back into a very ordinary kind of life. That need not happen to you. But it could. You should face that possibility.

The antidote for that event is to cultivate compassion in your mind every day. If you move along the path of Buddhadharma and become overworked by it, thinking, "I just can't practice that many hours a day. I cannot do this activity that propagates the Dharma anymore. It's just too much." If you become dry inside, if you think you just can't go on, there's only one way that that could happen to you. You have forgotten the suffering of others.

You must cultivate the memory that even in this visible world where beings can be seen, there is suffering that you cannot comprehend. You must think that there are children being abused everywhere, that there is starvation and poverty. You must think about the terrible diseases that afflict the body, speech and mind. You must think about the horrible things that come along with suffering, and the depth of suffering that exists, even in the realms that you can witness. If you think about that everyday, more about that than you do about yourself, you will not fall off the path of Dharma. When you become weak, when you waiver, that is when you forget. That is when you think the path is all about you. It's when you forget that you are practicing for their sake, and that you are practicing also to liberate your mind so that you can be of benefit to others.

A non-Buddhist practitioner might say, "I've got another idea. Why don't I do what I know how to do best. I'll go out and make some money, and then I'll feed everybody. I can do that."

I'll tell you a story about when I went to India. In our innocence, we thought, "Let's go see Bombay; this is really going to be great." So we got in a taxi and we went through the streets of Bombay thinking that we were going to see the India on the postcards. What I saw were streets so filled with sickness—leprosy, deformity, unbelievable poverty—that I couldn't see anything else. I know there were beautiful buildings. I know there was beautiful scenery, but I couldn't see those things.

Every time the taxi stopped, people with only part of a limb and open sores of leprosy would stick their arms in the car and beg. Mothers would hold up their babies that they had done something to, saying, "Help us, help us." So I started passing out dollar bills to everyone. I soon realized I was in deep trouble as I only had a limited amount of money, but that didn't stop me.

I was traumatized by this. I was crying to the depth of my heart, because I had known that suffering existed, but I was used to my brand of suffering. I had never seen anything like this. I continued to pass out dollar bills, and finally the taxi driver stopped. He turned around and said, "Lady, don't do this anymore. What is one dollar going to do for these people? Maybe they'll eat today. What will you do for them tomorrow? And if you give out one dollar to everyone you see, there are so many people like them in India, you couldn't help them all." His saying that shocked me; he was right. Even if I could manage to become wealthy, I couldn't feed the world. And hunger is only one kind of suffering. How can you help the other kinds of suffering? This kind of ordinary compassion ultimately does no good.

Why are those people suffering in India, and why were you born here in the West where things are relatively comfortable? Why are there animals and why are there humans? Why are there other realms of existence? Why is there so much suffering in one place, and much less suffering in another place? It is because of karma. That is the reason for all of this. Yet there is a cure for negative karma, which is the kind of karma that causes suffering. Ultimately, it is the only cure that will work. That cure is the eradication of hatred, greed and ignorance from the mindstreams of sentient beings. And the root of hatred, greed and ignorance is desire.

This doesn't mean if we see starving people we shouldn't feed them, that we should immediately teach them the Dharma. That, of course, won't work. We have to be skillful. If people are hungry, we feed them first, and then we teach them. But your job now is to do neither. You might not have money, and you might not have the ability to teach just yet. But you can do something. You can practice Dharma in such a way that you, yourself, become free of hatred, greed and ignorance. You can practice so that you can liberate your mind from cyclic existence for one reason and one reason only: that after liberating your mind, you can emanate in a form that will continue to benefit beings. You can liberate your mind from desire to such a degree that you have only one hope, and that hope is that you will be born again and again in a form that will bring this antidote to other suffering beings. That's what you can do.

Somehow you have found yourself in this fortunate, amazing position where this feast of possibility is laid before you. How did you come to this point? How is it possible that you have this option? You must have done something right in the past, and I suggest that you now build on it. If you don't cultivate the mind of extraordinary compassion and such a burning love that compassion is the most important force in your life, then the natural inclinations of a mind filled with desire will overcome you. This is Kali Yuga, the age of degeneration, and that's how it is. You must practice and cultivate that mind of compassion, of love, so thoroughly that you are moved to the core by even the faint possibility that you might achieve liberation in order to benefit beings. You think of nothing else. You must cultivate that until you burn with it. Don't be afraid of that kind of love.

In the West we are taught, "Be cool. Hey, I'm an intellectual, I don't think like that. I'm kind of special." That's what we're taught, that's our value system. That is the same value system we will take to our graves, and only the selfishness of that kind of idea will survive, not the intelligence. There is one thing that will survive this life, and will create the karma for your next life. It is the purity of your mind and the degree of love that you have accomplished. This will be the determining factor for how you will return time and time again in a form that will benefit beings until someday there is no more suffering.

I have listened to some of the teachings on Buddhist cosmology, and heard the prophecy that there will be a time when there is no Buddha in this world—no teaching, no help, and no light. When things will be so dark there will be nothing, no hope. As a Buddhist I am supposed to believe this teaching, and I try. But I refuse to accept it, I won't accept it, and if that makes me a bad Buddhist, then I am. But rather than think in a prideful way that I refuse to accept this teaching, I hope instead to cultivate an endless amount of energy to continue to practice for the benefit of others, no matter what the odds are. To consider that it is worthwhile if even one person can be benefited.

I wish we would all think in this way—that nothing will stop us. I find it necessary to believe that compassion is the strongest power anywhere, that love is stronger than prophecy. Believing this, we must continue as we are. Every day we must be stronger and continue in a more determined way.

When I see those of you who have taken ordination, I think you are the hope of the world. If you can remain emanating in the world always, even after attaining supreme realization, if your love is that strong that you change the prophecies, we have hope.

I also think of those who are newly starting, and those of you who are intermediate, and those of you who are choosing whatever particular path you choose. If you use the Buddha's understanding, and come to a point of profound commitment and practice—if you consider love is your life, so that it will increase throughout every future incarnation—then you, too, are the hope of the world.

We must take this vocation very seriously. I don't mean we have to walk around like somber people, with a terrible, woeful expression on our faces, or that we never get to have any fun anymore. It's not like that. But our sense of joy is the kind of joy that is born of the mind of compassion, the kind of joy that appears in the mind with the commitment to benefit beings at any cost, the kind of joy that knows there is an antidote to suffering. That kind of joy is stronger than human joy and human sadness, because those things come and go, day to day, up and down, in and out.

I suggest you choose to live a lasting life of love, rather than one that is impermanent and superficial. In doing so, come to know something that doesn't vary. Know something that grows from a tiny seed into a profound sense of bliss, which, as it grows, produces the kind of realization that can let you at last be someone who can truly help sentient beings with the right medicine.

You are at a crossroads in time now. Tremendous opportunities are coming your way. They have come your way. You are at a point very rare in cyclic existence. It is now possible for you to make this choice. It was not possible before. You should take this time very seriously, and consider deeply whether you will cultivate the mind of compassion every moment from now on for the rest of your life, and in all future lives to come, knowing that this is the only end to suffering.

Compassionate Action

*The only thing that is
meaningful is to make this life
a vehicle by which you can come
to benefit beings.*

One of the most important and central thoughts in Buddhist philosophy is the idea of compassion. The Buddha taught that we must cultivate our lives as a vehicle to be of benefit to all sentient beings. It's good that you're a good mother, and it's good that you're a good friend, but we can't limit ourselves to a small, familiar circle. We have to go on and on increasing our compassionate activity, our influence and our determination until we attain a level of kindness or compassion that supersedes what we believe is reasonable. We can't stop even with our nation. We can't think that we only want to help Americans. Nor can we stop with our world. We can't think that we only want to help humans and animals, which are the ones that we can see. We have to think, according to the Buddha, that we wish to be of benefit to all sentient beings.

A sentient being is one who has sensory feeling or the development of that kind of discriminating consciousness. According to the Buddha's teachings, there are six realms of cyclic existence, and there are sentient beings in all of these realms. The human realm and the animal realm are visible to us. This is living proof that at least some of the Buddha's teaching is right. We see human beings and we see animals; therefore, we know that they exist. But according to the Buddha's teaching, there are also non-physical beings and different kinds of beings that must be considered if we are to truly develop the mind of compassion.

Limiting ourselves to an identity such as,"I am a woman," or "I am a man," or "I am an American," or "I am a Russian," or even "I am a citizen of planet earth," is not the way of the Buddha. Instead, we should think that on every particle we can see, and all those that we cannot see, and in every inch of space, there are millions and millions of sentient beings. And space goes on forever. If we intend to develop the mind of kindness, it must extend to all sentient beings equal to the limits of space. Space has no limits and there are limitless beings, seen and unseen. Therefore, we must extend the mind of compassion to beings far beyond those we can conceive of with our brains. That is an awesome thought. How can we really do that? We think that must be impossible. How can we be directly concerned with somebody we can't see? How can we really care about something that might be infinitesimally small, like bacteria? Or a sentient being that may be as large as a galaxy? How can we seriously consider we must be kind to all sentient beings in that way?

When you develop the mind of compassion, you have to be careful how you develop that mind. If you examine yourself profoundly and honestly—and you have to be willing to be very honest with yourself—you may find that your goal is not really to benefit all sentient beings, but to be a kind person. There are worlds and universes of difference between these two goals. One is selfless: you truly wish to be of benefit to all sentient beings. The other is heading in the right direction, but ultimately it is not selfless because you wish that you could be a kind person. I hope that you can hear the difference between these two ideas. There are worlds of difference between them.

How does one cultivate the selfless goal and not fall unconsciously into the trap of ending up with the second goal? A good way to begin is to open our eyes and truly understand the nature of suffering. Why is there suffering in the world? Why is there suffering in the worlds unseen? If we don't examine this idea, we might take what we see at face value. We might look at people in poor parts of town and say, "Oh they're suffering because they're poor." We might look at people in different countries around the world and say, "Oh, they're suffering because they're hungry." We might look at people in different situations and think we understand the nature of their suffering. But we're looking at the symptom of their suffering. We're looking at the fact that they are suffering, but we still do not understand why.

If we see that they are suffering—that some people are poor, some people are hungry, some people are old, some people are sick, and some people are dying—and do not probe to understand the reason for their suffering, we might fall into the trap of trying to do something about those apparent issues. There's nothing wrong with doing something about those issues. In fact I hope you do, because human kindness—exemplary and virtuous human kindness—has to be part of this world, it has to be part of the activity that you, as Bodhisattvas, are involved in. But if you stop there, you will never succeed, because if you try to cure the symptom of suffering without going to the cause, it's impossible. The suffering will simply pop up in new and different ways.

In order to cure the symptom of suffering you might decide to manipulate the circumstances, or the environment. If you see people who are hungry, you give them food. If you decide you want to feed them for the rest of their lives so that they are never hungry, then you have to feed them three times a day, every day, for the rest of their lives, or teach them how to feed themselves. What are you going to do when they get sick? They will get sick. What are you going to do when they get old? They will get old. What are you going to do when they get lonely? What are you going to do when all the different kinds of discomfort pop up? What does it matter if you help a few people? What about the other 7.3 billion on the planet? What about the animals? Where will you start? What will you do, if your intention is merely to manipulate the environment so that the discomfort that you see is finished? Even if you have worked every moment selflessly and have given away all your money, and then have gotten money from other people to help, doing everything that you could to make these things happen, you wouldn't put a dent in it, not even the tiniest dent. Why? Because you are trying to manipulate something that is very superficial.

This apparent reality that we are viewing isn't that deep. It's nothing. It's a ghost. It's a puff-ball. We can't move it, because wherever we move it, it will appear somewhere else. We cannot manipulate our environment. We cannot manipulate phenomena and achieve any real lasting success. We can achieve temporary success. We can have the satisfaction of seeing someone fed who has been hungry, and that person can feel the satisfaction of a meal. If we fed people on a grand scale, it might be a grand satisfaction. But it is not permanent, it is not a solution, and the reason, according to the Buddha's teaching, is that hunger and poverty and loneliness are not the causes of suffering. They are the results or the symptoms of something else. According to the Buddha's teaching, the root causes of suffering are hatred, greed and ignorance.

We might take issue with that statement. Say we think about a hungry Indian child, or a hungry American child, or a hungry Ethiopian child. Sure, all of them probably do hate because they're hungry; and they probably are ignorant because they've never gone to school; and they probably are greedy. Boy, if you handed one a biscuit, he'd just grab it and run because he's so hungry. But we have to probe more deeply. We are only looking at a set of symptoms. According to the Buddha's teaching there is an underlying cause that makes phenomena appear as it does in any given situation, and that cause is karmic. The Buddha's teaching is that all phenomena arises from a cause, and that everything that is seen, felt, and heard is actually the emanation or the result of one's own mind. The mind itself produces all visible phenomena. I hope you can really hear that. To change suffering as it appears in the world can never be permanent. It can never do much good. What has to be done is to change the karmic background or cause and effect scenario of one's own mind. In doing so, you can hopefully come to a place where you can also be of benefit to others.

You cannot be a 'sugar daddy' in this world; there are no 'sugar daddies' in this world. You cannot be the conqueror or the savior as you cannot conquer someone else's mind. Each person has to relieve themselves of the hatred, greed and ignorance in their own minds. But you can be the savior, and you can be the conqueror, in the sense that you, yourself, can liberate your own mind from hatred, greed and ignorance. In so doing, you can be a way or a path or an instrument by which the hatred, greed and ignorance in the minds of others can also be liberated. Therefore, your prayers have to consist, at least in part, of liberating your own mind from the causes of suffering. At the end of every practice, at the end of every teaching, at the end of every empowerment or anything that you do as a Buddhist, the prayer is this: "May I attain liberation in order to benefit beings."

It's very difficult for Americans to hear this kind of thing. It is a real struggle. We don't like to hear about suffering; it's so hard for us to hear about suffering. Yet, if you go to different parts of the world, they know about suffering. They know it exists. There are lots of people in the world that can say, "Hey, I've heard about this. I know this song." But we who live comfortably don't like to talk about it. We think it's beneath us somehow to speak of suffering. We've become hardened to the idea.

You might say, "Well, I don't believe that it does any good to talk about suffering. I think it does good to think positive thoughts and to constantly create a positive world." I don't think that's the answer. We have become hardened to the idea of suffering, and we must first cultivate within ourselves a willingness to understand the nature of suffering so deeply and profoundly that we can do something other than scratch the surface.

It's almost impossible to attain the goal of selfless compassion, where you commit every fiber of your being to benefiting all sentient beings, seen and unseen, without a moment's hesitation. It's almost impossible to develop the kind of compassion where you understand that all sentient beings are revolving helplessly in such suffering that they can't bear it, and you can't bear to think it's going on, without cultivating a deep understanding of suffering. You want to avoid the trap of making the very same prayers that the selfishly motivated person might do, but instead have the idea that you want to be a great Bodhisattva.

One goal will produce lasting results and the other will not. The person with the motivation of selflessness has the key. Through extraordinary, selfless compassion, that person has the strength to persevere through everything until he or she is awake. That person will persevere until he or she has completely purged from his or her mind even the smallest, gossamer thin seeds of hatred, greed and ignorance. The person whose motivation is to be the 'good person' will not be able to do the same for any length of time. The foundation isn't strong enough. That person may need some kind of feedback, or warm fuzzies as reward for being good. Even tried and true Buddhists will find this impure motivation in their minds. Even our ordained Sangha will find that they, themselves, will have dry periods. You'll go spiritually dry, bone dry, and you'll think, "What am I doing here? I can't go on; it's just too hard." Then the next day, you'll wake up and you'll think, "Another day...good." You'll have all these different feelings that are just so common. Everybody, everybody has them. You don't have to be a Buddhist to have these feelings.

Why does it flip flop back and forth? Because you have not built the firm foundation of very pure, selfless compassion. You need to cultivate it every single moment. You need to get yourself past the point where you need warm fuzzies to keep you going. If you are only looking at the symptom of suffering and trying to manipulate your environment to turn suffering around, you will always need feedback. That feedback may or may not come. Your compassion, your love should not depend on that.

How can you develop the kind of love that sustains itself? How can you cultivate compassion like a fire that never runs out of wood to burn? That never goes out? The fire of compassion is based on being courageous enough to come to an understanding of suffering. You have to come to a deep understanding that all sentient beings are suffering endlessly and helplessly, and bring yourself to the point where you can't bear it. Cultivate the understanding that even though you know you can't see all sentient beings, you can't feel them, you can't touch them, still, you want nothing more than to rid hatred, greed and ignorance from their minds, because you understand this is the cause of their suffering. You understand the whole dynamics of suffering: why it exists, how it exists, where it exists, how it grows; and at that point you become deeply committed.

You can begin by renouncing the causes of suffering yourself. If you have not renounced the causes of suffering, you can't do a thing for anyone else, and so it takes a tremendous amount of courage. According to the Buddha, hatred, greed and ignorance in the mind are the causes of suffering. Hatred, greed and ignorance are preceded by desire. If there is no desire in the mind, there is no root from which these poisons can grow; there is no cause for hatred, greed and ignorance.

Where does desire come from? It comes from the belief that self-nature is real. According to the Buddha, if you believe that you are a self, if you believe in self-nature as being real, as being truly existent, then there has to be desire, because in order to be a self or to have a self, you have to define a self. That's how it is. If you believe in the nature of self, you have to have an underlying belief that self ends here and other begins there. You have to have some conceptualization in your mind about what the self is, because the idea of self cannot exist without some definition. Conceptual proliferation develops, and with that, desire.

Desires are not always fulfilled. There is always the contest between self and other, and from those contests the three root poisons of hatred, greed and ignorance occur. It is the presence of hatred, greed and ignorance in the mind that causes phenomena to appear as they do. If there were no hatred, greed and ignorance in the mind, there would be no cause for suffering and therefore we would not see the phenomena of war, hunger, old age, sickness and death in the world. There would be no cause. This is the understanding and commitment that you should think about and work with in your mind.

What form will your compassion take? Making compassion your root commitment to sentient beings must take some form. How can you begin to do that? First, I recommend again that you be courageous enough to study the nature of suffering: how it has evolved, what it means, where it exists. See for yourself. Go through a logical thought process. What will bring about the end of suffering? If I did this and this and this and this, will suffering really end? What can the possible results be? Allow yourself to really go through an examination of suffering. Come to your own understanding of suffering so that you can decide what your next action must be. Allow yourself to think, "Well, if I did this good thing for somebody, or if I fed the world and got everybody out of poverty, what would the result be?" Follow this line of reasoning to its logical end, and see if there's any specific action that you could take that would truly end suffering completely.

Then, think of the Buddha's logic and try to understand what that might mean. What if what the Buddha says is true? What if hatred, greed and ignorance are the root causes for suffering? What if you could completely remove the seeds of suffering from the fabric of reality? What if it were possible, through the extensive practices given by the Buddha, to accomplish that for yourself first, and then reincarnate in a form by which you could benefit others by offering that same method again and again? Might that be a solution? It's a slow one, but it's a big universe. Is it possible that might work? According to the Buddha's teaching, when you take a vow as a Bodhisattva, you vow to liberate your own mind from hatred, greed and ignorance. You vow to liberate your mind from the very idea of self-nature as being truly valid. You agree to liberate yourself from any form of desire, and you do that specifically so that you can return again and again, in whatever form necessary, in order to be of benefit to sentient beings. You agree to propagate the Dharma. It doesn't mean that you become a born-again evangelist. It means that you reincarnate and allow yourself to return in whatever form necessary in order to bring teachings to beings that will finally help them out of the sea of delusion that comes from the belief in self.

You should contemplate this and think, "Is this solution really useful?" You have a couple of different options at that point. If you decide that the Buddha's teaching is valid and useful, you can begin to develop aspirational compassion. Right now, if I were to say to you, "Do you want to help people? Do you want to help the world?" You'd say, "Yeah, I'm on! Look at what I've done. I've done a lot!" But I tell you, until we reach supreme enlightenment—and I'm talking about bona fide, rainbow-body, walk-on-the-water, supreme enlightenment—we must continue courageously to develop the mind of compassion in every moment. Until we can liberate the minds of others just through a breath, just through a glance, just through a moment of being with them, just through a prayer, we have not truly attained the liberating mind of compassion.

We must continue with this effort throughout all of our lives. Even though we may have the idea of compassion, we must develop aspirational compassion. We must aspire to be anything that would bring true and lasting benefit to beings. We must offer ourselves and our minds again and again and again. I think of one prayer of a Western Bodhisattva that touched me very much as a child, "Lord, make me an instrument of Thy peace." That's the kind of thought that we as Westerners must have within our minds. As we begin to become more comfortable with Eastern terminology, then we can think, "Let me be born in whatever form necessary, under any conditions in order that beings should not suffer. If there is the need for food, let me return as food. If there is the need for drink, let me return as drink. If there is a need for a teacher, let me return as the teacher. If there is a need for shade, let me return as the tree. If there is the need for love, let me return as arms." You must continue to develop this idea in such a selfless way that it doesn't matter to you in what form you can give this love.

Your job would be to liberate your mind to such an extent that you achieve realization through strenuous activity. Yes, the Dharma is difficult. Any path that promises to lead to enlightenment has to be difficult because it's a long way from here. Let's face it, any path that leads to bona fide, no-kidding, walk-on-the-water, rainbow-body enlightenment—I'm not talking about a psychological "a ha!," I'm talking about the real juice—must be very involved, very profound.

So your first thought must be, "Let me then liberate my mind to such an extent that I achieve some realization, and then I wish to return in whatever form is necessary. May I be able to emanate in many bodies. May these emanations fill the earth, and, if necessary, one-on-one, through those emanations, let suffering be ended. Or if it can be done in some other way, I don't care. It has no meaning to me. Only that suffering should end. What is important is that all sentient beings should themselves achieve liberation and go on to benefit others as well, until there are no more, until all six realms of cyclic existence are free and empty."

When you get up in the morning, think, "As I rise from this bed, may all sentient beings rise from the state of ignorance and may they be liberated until there is no more suffering." When you brush your teeth, think, "As I brush my teeth, may the suffering of all sentient beings be washed away." When you take your shower, think, "As I take this shower, may all sentient beings be showered with a pure and virtuous path by which they themselves can be liberated." When you walk through your door, think, "May all sentient beings walk through the door of liberation."

Everything that you do should have meaning. It's important that your life be understood as a vehicle for practice. It's the only thing that is meaningful: to make this life, which is so rich in opportunity, a vehicle by which you can come to benefit beings. This is the development of aspirational Bodhicitta. Every time you do something good, use that opportunity to dedicate it to the liberation of all beings. If you pat a little child on the head and it makes them smile, that's a good thing. So you must think, "I dedicate the virtue of this action to the liberation and salvation of all sentient beings." If you give money to somebody, pray, "I dedicate the virtue of this act to the liberation and salvation of all sentient beings." You should continue like that in everything that you do. Make up your own prayer. You don't have to use mine. Dedicate everything that you do so that it might go on, and grow, and be of use to benefit beings. Wean yourself from empty activity, activity that is useless and meaningless. Wean yourself from the need for 'feel-good' junk. Learn how to live a life in which your only concern is to liberate beings from the causes of suffering, because doing this is the only thing you can really feel good about. You aspire constantly through these prayers. You really train yourself to do this, and it should never stop.

After you are stable on the path of aspirational compassion, you have to think about concrete or practical compassion. You don't forget aspirational compassion, saying, "Oh, I did that for a little while when I was a younger practitioner." You should never stop. Never. I will never stop, and you should never stop. That's not baby stuff. That's the real stuff. Then you expand this to include practical compassion.

First you have to decide that the Buddha was right. You look at the Buddha's teachings and you say, "If he's right, then I have to think of some practical way to eliminate hatred, greed and ignorance from the world and from the mindstreams of myself and all sentient beings."

Based on that you begin, and your practice should be deep and true. If you choose to be a Buddhist, the path is laid out, and the path is secure. It goes all the way to supreme realization. If you choose not to be a Buddhist, you still have to find a way to live a life of practical compassion, based on the goal of rooting hatred, greed and ignorance out of the mindstreams of yourself and all sentient beings. You should think that reciting many prayers on a regular basis for others could be of use. You should think activities that cause you to realize the emptiness of self-nature and therefore eliminate desire from your own mindstream would be of benefit. And that, finally, free of desire, when you are truly awake, as the Buddha said, you can go on to benefit others. You should be determined to liberate your own mind, and you should pray every day that you will return in whatever form necessary in order to liberate the minds of all sentient beings.

Now, when we talk about practical compassion, it actually occurs on two levels. There's a universal level, in the sense you care so much for all sentient beings that your goal is to do whatever is necessary to eliminate suffering for them all. But does that mean that if you see a hungry child you shouldn't feed him? Or does that mean you shouldn't be kind in an ordinary, human way? Ordinary compassion, ordinary human kindness is very important. But in understanding the Buddha's teaching, it shouldn't be the only thing you do. You have to live an ordinary, virtuous life, but you have to live an extraordinary life as well. The activity of kindness and compassion should have both a universal and an ordinary level.

On the other hand, I don't believe in 'idiot compassion.' Have you ever heard of idiot compassion? It is when you look at people who are needy and you see them going through their stuff, and you try to be so kind to them and give them what they need, or what they say they need. You actually don't help them because you increase their dependency. You increase their willingness to tell you how much they need. You're just helping them along; you're playing with them. So I don't believe in idiot compassion because it doesn't help them. I believe that sometimes, real compassion has to be harsh.

In Buddhism, you see as many wrathful deities as you do peaceful deities. Why is that? Is it because the Buddha is half mean and half nice? I don't think so. It's because sometimes compassionate activity has to be a little wrathful. Sometimes it has to be a little aggressive. It depends. If you really are pure and your determination is to really be of benefit, and not just to be a nice guy, after training yourself in this way, you'll know what to do. You won't get hooked on idiot compassion. Everybody likes 'feel-good' stuff, but that doesn't always help. You should, however, be a human being of virtue. You should be kind. You should be honest.

To truly understand the mind of compassion is to understand suffering. To be willing to cultivate aspirational compassion and act in accordance with those aspirations, so that you fully intend to liberate your mind from the causes of suffering and fully intend to return in whatever form necessary in order to benefit beings. In so doing, you're on your way. Whether you call yourself a Buddhist or not, kindness is a universal term. No one's got a corner on it. Compassion is not a word that the Buddha invented.

I am a Buddhist because I found this religion is the most useful way to benefit beings. This is my own determination. If you also determine this for yourself, then continue to do what you're doing. Perhaps you're heading towards studying Buddhism, or perhaps you are already studying it. But if you don't want to become a Buddhist, that doesn't let you off the hook! You still have to live a life of compassion. No matter what path you're following, compassion is the only way to realization. No matter whom you're listening to, hatred, greed and ignorance are the causes for suffering. There is universality about all this. Whether you call yourself Buddhist or not, you still have a job to do. I suggest doing it by first cultivating the firm foundation of fervent aspiration to be of ultimate benefit, and by having the courage to look at the content and meaning of suffering and determining how best to overcome it.

Softening the Mind

Open your eyes and look around.
All sentient beings are suffering.

The precepts that the Buddha laid down are real and workable for everyone. You don't have to be a Buddhist to hold to these precepts. One of these is the realization that all sentient beings want to be happy, yet don't have the skills or knowledge to achieve happiness. Another is the realization that because of our ineptness at capturing that happiness we make ourselves sad. In fact, the Buddha teaches us that all sentient beings are suffering because we don't know how to attain happiness.

You don't have to be a Buddhist to notice this is true. You don't have to be a Buddhist to look around you, if you are willing to look with courageous eyes, and see that this is so, and you don't have to be a Buddhist to use the antidote. That antidote is purity of conduct. It is purity in practice, whatever your practice might be. The antidote is the realization of compassion, which should be the core of one's life. Of course, the Buddha's teaching is more involved than this, but still one does not have to be a Buddhist to hold to these teachings. They are universal.

If you have been studying Buddhism for some time, you may think you have already learned the Buddha's basic teachings that all sentient beings are suffering, that there is an antidote to suffering, that all sentient beings are trying to be happy, and that one needs to hold a compassionate viewpoint. But this is not true. You still need to hear these things.

No matter how long I teach, and no matter whom I teach, whether they are brand new to anything metaphysical, or whether they've gone on 20-year retreats, I will always address first and foremost the root reasons why one should practice. These basic beliefs are the foundational viewpoint that will encourage you to keep practicing, and, most especially, to keep practicing the idea of compassion.

There is never a time on your path when this is no longer necessary. In fact, the further you go on whatever path you choose— and specifically on the Buddhist path—you will meet up with challenges. You will invariably meet obstacles that make you feel tired and unwilling to go on. You will feel the pressures of living in the material world, especially living here in the West where we are so busy. It is a stretch to be a person committed to a spiritual path, whether it is the Buddhist path or not. It is a stretch because most of us have to earn a living and raise our families, and do all those things that are so time consuming. It is easy to fall back and say, "I'll wait until later. I will wait until I'm older and more settled, or less busy."

It is good to hear the Buddha's foundational teachings. You shouldn't think that if you've been a long-time Dharma student you are beyond all this. If you think that, then I have to tell you from my heart that you have a problem. I don't think that, and I don't know of any teacher who thinks that. Every teacher I have ever spoken to has told me to teach compassion first. Teach first the foundational teachings, and keep on that throughout your whole involvement with the Buddhist path.

In this book, we will continue with the idea of compassion because, as I have said, from the first day that I began teaching until the last day that I ever have the opportunity to teach; I will invariably speak of compassion. If compassion were ice cream, by the time you finish with me you will have tasted every flavor at least 475 times. So, now we will talk about another flavor of compassion.

Previously, we have discussed why compassion is necessary. Then we spoke about how to begin to apply that compassion. We talked about various ways in which one could be motivated by compassion, as well as thoughts that you might have found moving or encouraging and that were geared to deepen and soften your mind. These are very important. One of the greatest, most precious jewels that you will hopefully attain in traveling the Buddhist path, or any spiritual path, is to have your mind softened and deepened.

There is an expression in one of our prayers, that one's mind becomes 'hard as horn.' The minute I first read that particular phrase, it touched me deeply. Every time I have thought about it, it has meant more and more to me. One's mind becomes hard as horn because of the discrimination, the conceptualization that is involved with the idea of ego, because of the pride and arrogance that arise from our belief in self-nature as being inherently real. We have established in our minds all of the clothing, the dogma, the discrimination of this idea of self as being real. These things become rigid in our minds, and our minds are no longer gentle.

The moment you decide in some subconscious way you have an ego, that you are a self, you have to start gathering the constructs of self-identity around you. You have to determine where self ends and other begins. In order to do that your mind has to be filled with conceptualization. In order to be a self you have to survive as a self. In order to maintain this conceptualization that makes survival possible, your mind has to become rigid. So if I say to you that your mind is rigid, you shouldn't think I have insulted you. I am talking about a condition all sentient beings have, and it is a condition that is the cause of a great deal of suffering.

When I say that all sentient beings are suffering, I don't wish it to be a real downer for you. That is not the point. Realizing all sentient beings are suffering is meant to soften your mind, because to realize all sentient beings are suffering, you have to be willing to examine phenomena and to examine yourself in a deep way, in a way that you don't normally do. Therefore, you have to challenge your concepts. Why is that? Because naturally, and without any teaching or any encouragement, you will try to convince yourself that you are happy.

You may do this in much the same way that a person who is hungry and unable to eat will do something to take his mind off his hunger. Let's say its 10 o'clock. You're on the job, you're famished, and you know you can't get off for lunch until 12 o'clock. You are going to try to think of something else. You're going to try to keep your mind busy, or try not to focus on your hunger. In much the same way, if you are suffering and you don't have the technology to remove from your mind the causes of this suffering, you are going to try to convince yourself that you are okay. You are going to put a band-aid on it, and in order for you to do so, your mind has to become more hardened.

It is useful to really look around at sentient beings and see they are suffering. It is also useful to look at yourself. This is not meant to make you depressed or sad. It is meant to give you what it takes to go to the next step, which is to try to determine for yourself the way to remove the causes of suffering.

Even though there are times when hunger is not comfortable, when you would rather not think about it, there are also times when hunger is useful in that it keeps you alive. In the same way, while it may be uncomfortable for you to think that all sentient beings are suffering, it is actually quite useful for you to realize that. It is this realization that will give you the foundation and the ability to turn your mind in such a way that you have to seek out the causes of suffering, and how you can remove them from your mind.

It is not useful in any long-term way to try to convince yourself, by putting a band-aid on an ulcer, that everything is okay, because you still have to face the same things that you've always had to face. Nothing has changed. You still have to face old age, sickness and death. Neither does it help you to be helpful to other sentient beings. Look at the animal realm. Go to India and see how the oxen are beaten and tied up in order to be worked. They are worked all of their lives. That is suffering. Look at all the different ways that other creatures suffer just out of ignorance, because they have no way to help themselves.

Once you have determined suffering does exist, there is no need to dwell on it in a morbid way. Rather, you should think, "This is how it is. Now I have to realize that there is, in fact, a cure, there is a way to deal with this." It is not useful to dwell on suffering without also accepting the antidote. In other words, if you just think about hunger all the time, and you don't eat, that is stupid. When hunger is no longer useful to you, it is simply suffering. You should use your awareness of suffering to prod you to seek and practice the antidote to suffering. Use your awareness; it is your tool.

The Buddha says that all sentient beings are suffering and that enlightenment is the cessation of suffering. But we forget that enlightenment is the cessation of suffering. As a Buddhist you say, "Oh, yes, I've learned that. I practice the Four Thoughts that Turn the Mind. Enlightenment is the cessation of suffering. I have that memorized." Oh, really? I must ask you then, why do you still practice the technology of suffering? Because until you achieve supreme realization you are still practicing the technology of suffering. You realize this, and yet you continually create the circumstances that make you suffer. Here is why we do that: we have forgotten the other infallible law, the law of the certainty of cause and effect.

We have a problem. We are locked in to our own limited perspectives. We are in finite bodies, therefore our minds perceive in a finite way, a way that is natural for a finite reality to be perceived. Within this context, we can see that certain cause and effect relationships are absolutely unchangeable, that they always happen, that they can't be messed with. We can see that if we pick something up and then drop it, it will fall.

Now, you may say that cause and effect doesn't always work. There is magic, there is prayer, there are miracles. Okay then, pick something up, anything, and drop it, and stop it from falling. Let me see you do it. Who can do it? If you can do it, then I am going to buy your story and the class is over. Until we can figure out how to do that, it is certain if something is dropped, it will fall. It is also certain if you stick your hand in fire for long enough, your flesh will burn. It is certain if you never eat you will starve. It is certain if you catch a disease you will be sick. These things we understand.

It is also certain that everybody gets old. But the strange thing about us is, while we are still young enough to have a little twinkle in our eye, we will continue to convince ourselves that we will never get old. What we do is unbelievable. I have done it myself, so I know. Each year we buy something new, a little wrinkle remover, a little under-eye cover-up, and each year we still convince ourselves that nothing has changed. Then eventually, none of that stuff works. Then we have two choices: we can either face the facts or consider surgery. Whatever we do, we are putting off the inevitable.

Did you ever watch yourself when you were young? Did you see what you did? Do you watch young people now? Look at the teenagers you know. They are invariably right. They know everything. I knew everything at that age, too, so I understand. They know beyond everything. If there is more than everything, they know it. They have all the answers.

We are also like that. We are locked within a time-and-space grid. When we drop something, it falls, immediately. What makes it so immediate? If it were to hang in the air for ten years, then fall, invariably we would convince ourselves it's never going to fall. But since it falls immediately, since when we stick our hands in the fire, it hurts immediately, we believe that. Old age, sickness and death we don't believe. We sort of get it, but it's in the back of our minds somewhere.

Why is it we don't fully believe in cause and effect, even though we take into account the passage of time? It's because we are trying to be happy, so we convince ourselves that cause and effect is not absolute. Why is that? How is it that we can understand that we create the causes of suffering in our mind, and yet still convince ourselves it will not bear the fruit of suffering? It's because karma appears to ripen in different ways. Karma can ripen immediately. If I drop something and it falls, this is karma ripening. I dropped it; it fell. Karma can also ripen in a different way.

Because of your belief that self-nature is inherently real, you have created the delusion of a self. Self has a beginning and it has an end, and that is the cause for death. The cause for death is the belief in self-nature as being real; that is why people die. Yet you will convince yourself it is okay to believe in self-nature, that there is no problem as long as you can find a way to make self happy. You think it's going to be okay. But you are still going to die. We are doing this to ourselves, and we don't even realize it. The self is a finite thing. It had a beginning, a time when it was conceived. There was a time when the thought of self-nature as being inherently real first manifested. Since that is so, then it also must end. If there is a beginning, there is an end.

In the same way, we are constantly engaged in creating things that are the karmic causes of our own suffering, but we don't make a connection. The reason we don't make a connection is due to the other kind of karmic ripening, the one that you don't see in this life. The karma that ripens after a long time, an intermediate time, or even a short time, are karmic ripenings that you actually do not see in this lifetime.

Here then is a problem. Here is one of the reasons why it becomes very difficult to realize the unchangeable truth that all sentient beings wish to be happy, and yet not realizing how to create the causes of happiness, create instead the causes of suffering.

Many of the things that we have suffered in this lifetime seem to have been put upon us in an innocent way. We were innocent. Why is someone born with a cleft palate? Why are some of us born with a crippling condition, some handicap? Why do some of us become ill or die when we have tried to live a good life, when we have done everything we can to be kind to other human beings and have never killed anyone? It is because many of the causes that we see in this lifetime have come from a time before.

Now, from my point of view, if you don't believe in reincarnation you have no access to the technology of Buddhism. You have to accept the idea you have lived before, and that some of the results you see ripening in your life now are ripening due to causes created in a time you do not know. And that some of the causes you are creating now—because you are creating causes constantly—will ripen in a time you can not see. If you don't accept that, Buddhist or not Buddhist, you cannot evolve in your mind; you cannot adapt and have the strength to continue. In fact, you cannot have the perspective to practice the antidote to suffering. Everyone who has ever been considered a living Buddha on this earth has taught reincarnation. So maybe you might want to consider it an idea that you could adopt.

Cause and effect are infallible. They are 100 percent infallible. The reason I think this bears mentioning is that again and again I have seen practitioners, even those who have practiced Buddhism for a long time, do things they know will cause suffering, or even cause them to fall off the path and end their quest to follow the Buddha's teaching. I see them create nonvirtue constantly.

People trick themselves. Once they know that non-virtue is the cause for suffering, because there is a karma that ripens from the seed of non-virtue, they tend to create non-virtue in a sneaky way, thinking no one will ever know. They'll say things like, "I'm a Buddhist. I really can't kill. I've taken this vow. I'm wearing these robes." And, whap! They'll swat a mosquito. Or even more subtle than that, they'll make judgments thinking, "No one knows what's going on in my mind. No one will know." But they are constantly judging, and they think it will never bear fruit.

According to Buddhist teaching, and according to what I have seen, karma never fails to ripen. What you have done is create a non-virtue, and that non-virtue grows like a seed in your mindstream. It is an absolutely unchanging law that non-virtue will ripen in some way. The reason why you think you are getting away with judging others, for example, is because that seed may not ripen now. It may ripen ten years from now when you won't remember what you thought about that person. Or it may ripen next week, and you know how much you remember from last week! Or it may ripen in the next life, in which case there is no possible way that you could remember. But invariably, it will ripen.

In this way, the Buddha's teaching is born out. Even though we know all sentient beings are suffering, that the cessation of suffering is enlightenment, and that all sentient beings want to be happy, we still don't know how to create the causes of happiness. Through non-virtuous actions we continue to create suffering instead. Even though we have these concepts memorized, strangely, we still manage to create non-virtue continuously. Therein lies the schism, the schizophrenia, the craziness that we have: while we continue to yearn for happiness, and yearn for a life and a mind state that can only be the result of a complete absence of non-virtue, we continue to create non-virtue. It is psychotic. It is really schizophrenic. You are not in touch with reality when you act this way. You are not creating your life in a way that you truly want to live.

The problem lies in our lack of understanding of cause and effect. You need to convince yourself completely, as though it were written in cement in your mind, that cause and effect are infallible. Find a way to know this as deeply and instinctively as you know that if you stop breathing, your body will expire. Know this on such a profound level that it manifests like an instinct. Strive to internalize these ideas to such an extent that they never leave you, and that your mindstream is pregnant with them. Strive, so that you cannot consider creating non-virtue for even one moment.

Now, brothers and sisters, this is a tall·order. But for that reason, it is necessary to study the Buddhist truth, and you don't have to be a Buddhist to do it. You just have to look around. Open your eyes and look around. All sentient beings are suffering. But unfortunately, until your mind is softened and gentled through realizing that all sentient beings are suffering—that you yourself are suffering—you will never be able to convince yourself of the infallibility of cause and effect, because you will never consider that it is useful to consider the infallibility of cause and effect.

You only have to consider the suffering of sentient beings long enough to help you create within yourself a virtuous mindstream. Once you have created a virtuous mindstream, you no longer need consider suffering. It is not useful to suffer considering suffering. It is only useful if it compels you on a path that ends suffering. That is the point.

Having heard this teaching, I hope you never become weary hearing your teachers talk about suffering. You will only hear about suffering long enough for you to soften your mind and change the way you live. You will only hear about it long enough to fill your life with virtuous and compassionate acts. If you are not completely convinced that all sentient beings are suffering, you can't help them. You won't help them. You won't have the strength or the fortitude to persevere. But once your mind is stable in the practice of compassion, once you are moved by compassion to where it is a fire in your heart and you can't do anything except that which will end suffering, that which will bring enlightenment to all sentient beings, you don't need to meditate on suffering anymore. You are already on fire. Once you are convinced of the infallibility of cause and effect, to the extent that there is no more non-virtue in your mindstream, you don't need to think about suffering anymore. There is no point. You are already doing what is necessary to end suffering. However, once you are so filled with compassion that your whole life is virtuous, your whole life is a vehicle for nothing but compassionate activity, and once you are convinced of the infallibility of cause and effect to the extent that there is no more non-virtue in your mindstream, you are also enlightened!

The point is this. You are receiving this teaching for a certain reason. You might think you are just curious, or interested in Buddhism and would like to explore it a little further. Or you may think you would like to deepen, or you would like to learn all things from all places. Or you may be interested in becoming a Buddhist. Whatever your particular format, you do have a reason, and I bet that reason is based upon the fact that you want to find a way out of suffering not only for yourself, but for all sentient beings as well. When I say 'out', I don't mean that you want to get enlightened and then leave. I mean that you want to find a way out of the kind of mindstream, the kind of phenomena that causes suffering in both you and in all sentient beings. You want to see if there is another option.

Even if you haven't faced that fact exactly in your heart, you are looking for something, and you are a good person. You wouldn't be receiving this teaching if you were not a good person. You must be interested; you must have karma with the idea of compassion. Because of the infallible way that karma works, you could not receive this teaching if you didn't have the karma of compassionate activity. You must have a tremendous amount of virtue squirreled away somewhere. I am not claiming I am such a virtuous teacher that you have to be particularly virtuous to hear me. That is not what I am saying. I am saying that in order to hear the word 'compassion,' in order to hear the word 'Bodhicitta', in order to even hear these ideas from any source, you have to have a tremendous amount of virtue, because that is the Buddha's teaching.

You are at the beginning. You have arrived at the door to liberation. You are knocking on a door that opens to the end of suffering. You have a tremendous capacity here, and in order to utilize that capacity you have to begin to utilize the technology being offered you. That technology is very simple: You have to soften and turn your mind. Whether you are a Buddhist or not, in order to achieve any realization at all—in fact in order to continue in a steadfast way on a path without being pulled away by the craziness of your own mind—you have to develop stability. That stability has to be based on the softening and gentling of your mind. You have to free it as much as possible from discursive thought, and from the conceptualization associated with the belief in self-nature as being real. You have to free it enough to be able to get some perspective.

Through that stability and deepening we can begin to examine these essential thoughts: that all sentient beings want to be happy, that all beings are suffering, that there is a cessation to suffering, and that the cessation to suffering is called enlightenment.

We should examine these thoughts, because Westerners have a very complicated world. Maybe it is hard to understand that all beings wish to be happy here in the West, because here we listen to the news and we hear about people throwing bombs at each other. We hear about robbery, rape and murder. We think, "Wow, that person raped and murdered; he is a horrible person." We condemn him immediately and forget the other side of that thought, which is that he is trying to be happy. Can you believe that? Is that not an awesome thought? People who are raping and murdering, people throwing bombs in each other's windows—how can you believe that these people want to be happy? Yet, it is absolutely the case. All sentient beings want to be happy, but they are drunk with the idea that there is no cause and effect. They are drunk with the idea that they can attain happiness by manipulating their environment in some crazy way. It just doesn't work.

For instance, a freedom fighter might believe if he destroys a thousand people by throwing a bomb into a building, he might attain some liberty for his people, and through that effort he will be happy. That might be his thinking, but he doesn't realize he has killed a thousand people, and through his action has created the karma in his mindstream of a thousand deaths that can only be the cause of suffering. He really believes he is doing something good. Even the rapist and murderer—maybe he has an uncontrollable urge that is deep and profound. Where does that urge come from? Why don't you have it? It is because he has the karma of that urge. Maybe it was caused when many lifetimes ago he threw a bomb in somebody's window and killed a thousand people, and maybe that is why he has that urge in his mindstream now. So what does he do? He continues to rape and murder. At the moment of doing so, he thinks he will end the suffering of his uncontrollable urge through raping and murdering just once more.

That is how horrible it is, but these people really are trying to be happy. Think about that. Think about how they are suffering uncontrollably, revolving again and again in cyclic existence, helplessly, because of the karma that has infected their minds. They are helpless in the midst of the cause and effect that they have created, simply helpless. Even in these horrible cases it is true, all sentient beings are trying to be happy. On the other side of this law, which the Buddha declared, is that not understanding how to create happiness, they constantly create the causes of suffering through non-virtue.

These are things you absolutely must remember. You have to allow them to deepen your mind. They have to become as instinctive and natural to you as breathing. If you understand the infallibility of cause and effect to such a profound extent that it begins to change the compulsion you have to create non-virtue and therefore the causes of unhappiness, then you are a practitioner. You are practicing a technology that will lead you to realization. Whether you consider yourself a Buddhist or not, you are practicing a valid technology, a spiritual technology.

If you realize as well that all sentient beings are suffering, and are then motivated to examine the other side of that law—that enlightenment is the cessation of suffering—and therefore commit yourself to attaining enlightenment in order to end the suffering of yourself and others, then you are a practitioner. Whether you call yourself a Buddhist or not, you are a practitioner.

If you realize the belief in self and in the ego configurations that surround self—the rigidity, the need for survival, the hardening of the mind—are the causes of suffering, and begin to eliminate them by living a compassionate life, purifying your clinging to ego, then whether you call yourself a Buddhist or not, you are a practitioner of the highest caliber.

As a practitioner, you should consider these things: the idea of compassion, of living selflessly, of living an extraordinary life solely to benefit beings, to end their suffering, to bring about a situation in which they can create the cause of happiness rather than the cause of non-virtue. If you can live an extraordinary life, not only are you purifying your mind—because that is the antidote for self-absorption, and self-absorption is the cause of suffering—but you are also a contributor to a very precious idea: the idea of a world, of all worlds, free of pain.

These things you can consider. You can consider them in accordance with Buddhist teaching, or you can consider them separate from Buddhist teaching, even though they are not. You can consider them from whatever angle you wish. But I hope from my heart that whoever you are, and whatever your game plan is, that you will consider these things to the extent that your mind will be softened, and that you can adopt the two ideas that are foundational in the Buddha's path: renunciation and compassion.

What is renunciation? Do you have to give up your car? No, I have a car, and I have no plan to give it up. Do you have to give up a nice place to live? No, you don't have to give up a nice place to live. What then do you have to give up? You have to give up self-absorption. You have to give up selfishness. You have to give up a life filled with non-virtue. That is true renunciation, regardless of the outer form or appearance. You may choose to adopt the outer form of renunciation [ordination], which is a time-honored, pure and useful way to utilize these teachings. But you can also adopt it in an inner way. If you have the ability to practice renunciation in an inner and profound way, it is also useful. It also works.

What you renounce is self-absorption, and you begin to live an extraordinary life, one that is involved in Bodhicitta, or compassion. That is the way to understand Bodhicitta in the simplest view, to understand it as compassion. You must live an extraordinary life, and in living an extraordinary life you are actually taking the cure, you are taking the medicine. Not only is it a nice thing to do, not only will you be known worldwide as a nice guy, but you will also be taking the medicine of selflessness. If the sickness is the belief in self-nature and the desire and grasping that come from all the phenomena surrounding the idea of self, then the cure is a selfless life. The cure is compassion, and you are taking the cure.

I hope you think about all of these ideas, and that you think of them in such a way that you allow them to soften your mindstream, so that your mind is no longer hard as horn. Think about that phrase: our mindstreams are as hard as horn. If you adopt all of these things truly and deeply, with depth and love, and with courage—the lack of courage is what keeps us from taking it to the bottom line—you will be an excellent practitioner. Whether I ever see you again or not, whether or not you ever study other Buddhist teachings, you have the first and most important step.

The difference between a non-Buddhist and a Buddhist is that a Buddhist actually accepts these ideas, then goes beyond that to adopt the technology. There is a technology that comes specifically on the Vajrayana path. There is a whole pattern and set of profound practices that can cause you to accomplish the things I've talked about: to develop the life of Bodhicitta, to develop the mind of renunciation, to create virtue as opposed to nonvirtue. If you go on to be a Buddhist you will learn the technology, and you are free to do that. I hope you do.

But even if you don't, if you just stick with these basic, simple teachings that are both provable and logical, if you will study the world, even as you see it, with courage, if you do only that, you are on your way, and you should be very happy.

Nature of Mind

All sentient beings desire happiness.

If we studied Bodhicitta, or the mind of compassion, every single day for the rest of our lives, we wouldn't even scratch its surface because it is so profound. There are many different levels at which we might come to understand its meaning; the word Bodhicitta can't really be translated into English very well. It means enlightenment. It also means compassion. Compassion to us means something quite ordinary. We might think that we already understand compassion. We may think, "I don't eat meat anymore, and I try not to kill things. I try not to hurt anybody, and I feel sorry for most everybody, you know. Therefore I fully understand compassion." Unfortunately, if we think like that, we're probably missing a lot, and we fail to understand the real meaning of enlightenment. If we think we understand enlightenment the way most Americans do, I'm afraid we don't have a clear view of it, because we haven't had teachings on what that mind, which is free of conceptualization as well as discursive thought, is really like. We just haven't had that kind of teaching.

When we think of an enlightened being, we think of someone who dresses up a certain way. He or she wears robes and almost always has their eyes turned skyward. We have many different ideas about enlightenment and, unfortunately, none of them are true. The Buddhas and Bodhisattvas who are reported to appear in the world, for instance, take many different forms. They don't have to be a Buddhist to be a Bodhisattva; they just have to have realization. They take whatever form is necessary in order to benefit beings, because that is how the mind of compassion works. That is how the mind of enlightenment functions. It does not cling to the idea of self. It does not cling to egocentricity. Literally, a Bodhisattva might appear in the world as food or drink, offering its body in that way to benefit beings. It might appear in the world as a teacher. It certainly might do that. It might appear in the world as an ordinary, funky-style person. I mean funky beyond belief! Unless you have traveled in India and Nepal, you don't know what funky means yet! A Buddha or a Bodhisattva might appear in such a way that is funky beyond belief, and yet within the context of that life, has an incredible impact on many people, or on just two or three people who themselves go on to achieve realization and have an incredible impact on beings.

You see, the mind of the Bodhisattva is such that it doesn't cling to the idea of greatness. There is no thought of greatness. The moment we think we have to be great, or have to wear a certain kind of robe, or look a certain way, or do a certain dance, we have lost the entire idea and the main reason why a Bodhisattva would wish to incarnate in the world. A Bodhisattva's only purpose is to benefit beings, and that is done without attachment to form and content. It is done in whatever way is necessary.

If we wish to enter onto the path of a Bodhisattva and become that which benefits beings, we must have a heart that yearns for compassionate activity. We must want to help, or we wouldn't be able to receive teachings like this. This being the case, the first thing we have to do is let go of the concepts we have about how cool we are going to be when this process is finished. We cannot hold on to the rigid kind of thinking that honors only self. We must think of others.

How many of you are there? One, right? Look down, how many do you count? It's easy. So far as you know, there is only one of you. Now look around at the human beings in your immediate environment. Then think about all the human beings on this earth: 7.3 billion, at least. If your mind is really that of a Bodhisattva, you couldn't think for a moment of going around telling others how great you are. You couldn't think for a moment that it could be in any way important that you do the dance, or sing the song, or appear in some certain way that satisfies you, because there's only one of you, and there are 7.3 billion of them. If you have a mind that's free of the attachment to self, free of the burden of believing strongly in self-nature, then you must realize that weighed against 7.3 billion human beings, you simply don't weigh very much.

If you really wish to fulfill the idea of a Bodhisattva that is free of attachment to ego, free of the delusion that self-nature is relevant and important, and if you really wish to consider living a life of compassion, then serving others must become more important than even your own life. It is not that you become like a martyr. We're not talking about the Christian concept of a martyr. It's really different than that. It's just mechanics. It's just logic. It's just math. There are more of them than there are of you, so they matter more. With that idea, you seek only to benefit others. That being the case, as an aspiring Bodhisattva, you must begin to examine what the mind of Bodhicitta really is. What is this mind of realization? How is it that we become so deluded with the idea of self?

In Buddhism, we explore the idea of suffering first. In that regard, Buddhism has been given a bad rap here in America. Many of the New Age philosophies support the idea that one should think only positive thoughts, and use affirmations. "Just resolve your conflict in a very loving way." "Live a life that is free of conflict." "Try to keep your mood elevated." "Be happy all the time." The idea, according to many of these systems, is that if you have happy thoughts and meditate on happiness all the time, you somehow will be happy all the time.

Buddhism has a different approach. We shouldn't think that because it has a different approach, it has a different goal. Basically, according to the Buddha's teaching, all sentient beings want to be happy. That is something that you have to understand before you do anything in the Buddhadharma. Before you do any kind of studying, you have to meditate on the fact that all sentient beings desire happiness. Because we don't realize that. We forget. We tend to blame and judge and hate, because we forget that all sentient beings desire happiness, but they don't know how to be happy. They don't know how to create the causes for happiness.

This is not different from what New Age people think. They think that everyone has the right to be happy, and that we should try to be happy. But the Buddha's approach is slightly different, and it goes something like this: All sentient beings desire happiness, but are constantly creating the causes of unhappiness. Witness this is so by the fact that everybody you know has periods of unhappiness, if not constant unhappiness. That being the case, we must be creating the causes of unhappiness. Unhappiness doesn't come out of the clouds. It doesn't manifest out of nowhere. It has a cause. There is a cause and effect for everything.

The approach, then, is to study suffering and how suffering comes about, as well as how all sentient beings essentially are suffering. We can't understand how we create the causes of suffering, and we can't understand what the antidote to suffering might be, if we don't accept the fact that sentient beings are suffering. If we gloss over it, it gets away from us. The Buddhist approach to happiness is to study suffering in order to understand what the antidote might be. A Buddhist would say that if you go around saying affirmations and thinking positive thoughts all the time, perhaps it won't work as well as you would like.

A New Age thinker believes the superficial level of conscious thought, and the resultant underlying thoughts, cause unhappiness. The Buddha, however, says what causes suffering and discomfort is something far beyond the level of thought, and therefore cannot be excised simply through moderating your thoughts. It can be modified by thought, but the root of the causes of suffering cannot be removed. One has to go much, much deeper than that. What actually causes suffering is the belief in self-nature as being inherently real. The belief in self-nature as being inherently real leads to clinging and desire, and it is desire that causes suffering.

Now, let's say the New Age thinker might agree with this. He might say, "Yes, if you get attached to things, if you grasp onto things, they'll cause suffering. I get that." The difference is that the Buddha says you have to go really deeply into understanding the nature of mind, into realizing the nature of the emptiness of all phenomena, and the emptiness of self-nature, in order to excise that desire. You have to go much deeper than just ordinary thinking.

The reason I am inclined to believe what the Buddha taught is, first of all, he beat the game. That's a really good sign, as far as I'm concerned. He beat the game and he attained supreme realization. Secondly, I know people who have adhered strictly, diligently, faithfully and loyally to New Age philosophy. If they get hit by a car, they will tell you it was fortunate, and they learned a great deal from it. That's fine. I'm not going to argue. But two broken legs is not a good way to learn. Whatever happens to them, they just tend to gloss over it, and the problem is, they're still suffering. They're still suffering! My personal feeling is they're in worse shape than they were before, because they have no means by which to get hold of the causes of their suffering. Whether they merely gloss things over, or force themselves to think in a certain way, they still get old, get sick and die. They are still helpless in the face of circumstances. I feel that it's necessary to go deeper and to think in the way that the Buddha thinks.

What then is the cause of suffering? Why do circumstances appear as they do? Why are there old age, sickness and death? Why are there six realms of cyclic existence? All forms of life are impermanent. All of them experience some form of suffering. Animals certainly do. Animals grow old, get sick and they die. They get run over by cars. They get worms. They get mistreated. They get hooked up to yokes and made to pull carts and things like that. If you think that teaching animals to think positive is going to be the answer, good luck! I hope that you can do that, and I hope that you reincarnate again and again as a great Bodhisattva who can teach animals to think positive so that they won't suffer anymore. But, it may not be possible. Like the suffering in the animal realm, we must think that there are other realms of existence where beings are also suffering.

What is the root cause that goes underneath and beyond the thinking and reckoning of the human mind? What is so ancient that it has existed for time out of mind, even before you could think? What is so old that you were born with the certainty you too will die? In order to uncover these mysteries, you need to examine the idea of suffering. Once you can answer these questions, you are free to explore the path of enlightenment. According to the Buddha's teaching, the real cause for suffering is the belief in, and clinging to, self-nature as being inherently real. And here is a little bit that is so embarrassingly superficial, you could call it the Kellogg's cereal box-top version of the nature of mind. Anyway, having made my apology and legal disclaimers, I will continue!

For the very idea of self to arise there has to be a division in which there appears to be a separation between self and other. In other words, the mind arises in such a way that it becomes divided at that time. In order for that division to exist in any form, even the most subtle form, that which considers itself to be self, with the impetus to divide, must begin to gather data around itself. In order to be a self, self has to be distinguishable from other. Different discriminating thoughts begin to form, and self begins to clothe itself.

Once self begins to clothe itself, a tension arises. There is a need to maintain self in order to distinguish self from other, because if at any moment self drops the conceptualizations that surround it, self becomes indistinguishable from other, and there is only suchness. Therefore, the idea of survival becomes important. With survival comes the idea of clinging. With clinging, comes desire. If there is self, then, there is other, and there must be cause and effect. It is at this level that cause and effect arises. In the natural state, the uncontrived state, there is no cause and effect.

The moment there is the consideration of self-nature, the reality of cause and effect, or karma, begins immediately to appear in the most profound way. From that point on, karma is very, very real. We should not kid ourselves, thinking that we can talk our way out of cause and effect. It is real. Self then, in order to become distinguishable from other, must have a kind of inter-reactive relationship. In order to maintain the idea of self, there has to be the distinction of self. There has to be an idea to formulate self more and more firmly, to form ideas around self. The only way to do that is to react for or against other. Self has to have something to bounce off of. That is the way the idea of self is formed.

As long as the idea of self exists, self will experience other with either attraction or repulsion. There is no other way to experience other. Whether it's subtle or not, even if you are a proponent of New Age philosophy, and are supposed to love everybody and have unconditional positive regard towards others, if you could really examine your mind with determination, courage, innocence and willingness, you would discover that you are either attracted to or repulsed by everything you see, no matter how you gloss it over. No matter what you say, the karma is still forming. That is how the consequences of one's life actually manifest: through that constant inter-reactive relationship, through that interplay, through attraction and repulsion, through desire. That's how it's possible for you to be born. That's how it's possible for you to do things you feel uncontrollably forced to do.

Even if we are so convinced that we know all of these teachings, don't we still get into trouble? Don't we find that we react to circumstances in a way that is not skillful? Don't we, in fact, on an on-going basis make everything worse? I mean, it's true, if we are honest with ourselves. Every time we react, we make things worse. Even when we can't see that we've made things worse, I'm telling you this is the truth: We are constantly compounding the karma of our own minds. Even if in retrospect, we could see that we should have been loving, and we should have been kind and good, blah, blah, blah, blah, still, we are compulsive about it. We are what we are. We are 'feeling junkies.' We are hooked on sensual experience. And we react to it.

What then is the answer? If all of this is true, and desire is the foundation of all suffering, then what if the Buddha is right? What if all suffering comes from the belief in self-nature? Will it do to pacify our minds with positive thinking? Will it do to walk around with the idea or the New Age philosophy saying, "Oh, I'm already enlightened because I understand I am the creator, or one." I'd have to say you're talking about two selves there. You're talking about 'creator' and 'I,' and so long as there is distinction, so long as there is the belief in self-nature, you still have desire. You still have attraction and repulsion. You still have hope and fear. You haven't gone yet into a deep and profound understanding of the emptiness of self-nature. Of course, we have to do that through meditation. There is no ordinary language or ordinary experience that will teach us that profound understanding.

The best thing to do, actually, is to find a qualified teacher who can begin to help you, not only in terms of giving you the words—the verbal teachings—but also some kind of virtuous or valuable energy transmission. On the Vajrayana path, that is done through the transmission of the lineage. The teachings on the nature of emptiness, the teachings on the generation-stage practices, all of the different teachings that we receive here, are passed down through a lineage. That lineage originates in the mind of enlightenment, in the primordial state. It then is transmitted to us. It doesn't stop there. The minute we receive an empowerment, we're not going to instantly become enlightened. I wish it were that easy, but it is not. At that point, we are qualified to practice, and it is through the practice and our meditation—with the help of the transmission of the lineage—that we will achieve results.

Let's say you're not up to following a qualified teacher. Let's say you don't go that route. You can still meditate. You can still follow those basic precepts that are brought to us through the enlightened mind of the Buddha without going that route, if you wish. You may wish to bite off a small piece, and then see if you want another piece. There's no problem with that. You might realize some of the basic teachings, such as all sentient beings are suffering; there is an antidote to that suffering, which is supreme enlightenment. When we reach enlightenment there is no conceptualization of self, therefore there is no desire. Therefore, there is no discursive thought. Therefore, there is not the cause that creates the effect of suffering.

You must also realize that all sentient beings desire happiness, no matter what they are doing. Even if they are robbers, rapists and murderers, and they are doing things that look to you like all they're trying to do is hurt people. They are confused. They have the karma of murder in their minds. They are completely deluded. They are whatever you want to call them. But in their deluded way, in their feverish way, they too desire happiness. All sentient beings desire happiness. Yet, all of us, whether we are murderers, rapists and robbers, or if we are the nicest little New Age flower children you have ever seen in all your bliss-ninny days—we are just so sweet and we walk around with flowers in our hair and only eat vegetables and tofu—even if we are like that, we are still creating the causes for unhappiness. I'm giving it to New Age people, but I'm just making fun. It's no big deal. I've been known to eat tofu on occasion also! Anyway, even if you're that kind of person, you are still creating the causes for more suffering. You know that's true, because while you may not be murdering anybody, if you look at your life and look at the probability of the continuation of your life, you will at some time be sick, you will certainly age, and you will certainly die. There will certainly be circumstances you cannot avoid describing as suffering.

In order to get to the depth of this awareness we can begin to practice as the Buddha practiced. We can begin to take the antidote for desire. We can begin to take the antidote for the belief in self-nature as being inherently real. Therefore, the antidote will also be applied to the clinging and the reactive relationship of hope and fear, the attraction and repulsion syndrome, which is the mother of karma and circumstance. These are what cause circumstance and they will be eliminated.

How should we apply the antidotes? First of all, by living a life that is as selfless as possible and by beginning to purify our minds in such a way that we really honestly examine ourselves. Just how much of an ego do we have, anyway? If we can sit there and think, "Oh God, such an ego, you can't believe it!" If we can do that, then we're on our way, and we probably have less of an ego than the next person. If we're truthful with ourselves, we'll discover that any one of us has an ego that is so enormous, we're surprised we can fit in a room. We have to begin to examine ourselves as carefully, diligently and purely as we possibly can.

How do we do that? Do we just sort of go through our stuff and process it? No, I don't think so. I don't think the thing to do is to process it and be sorry that we have a big ego. What we want to do, actually, is to begin to practice in such a way that we say, "Okay, I have this ego. I want to apply the antidote." What is the antidote? The antidote is to strive to constantly live a life in which my welfare becomes less important—because I am only one—than the welfare of others, who are many. Again, it doesn't mean you roll your eyes heavenward, become extremely thin and become a martyr. I don't think that is the answer. The answer is that you live a life in which you consider how you can best benefit beings. You can start by aspiration, the aspiration to be truly compassionate. If you don't have the technique, if you don't know what to do first, begin through prayers of longing.

Do you remember the innocent sense of longing you felt when you first started to seek the spiritual path? You must have felt it at one point or another, or you could not receive this teaching. You could not. You must have longed to purify suffering. You must have longed to be of benefit to someone, sometime. You must have longed to attain the end of suffering, and there must have been the desire to do that in order to help others. It has to be.

Remember how happy you were when you felt that innocence,

that beautiful longing? There was a time when you were really happy when you thought that. Now, of course, we're too sophisticated. We're on the path, and we're already practitioners. So we tend not to continue with that thought in our minds, but we should. We should constantly, with great longing, make prayers in that direction. That's how you begin aspirational Bodhicitta. You begin to make prayers of longing: "I long to benefit beings. I pray with all my heart that I can take whatever form necessary in order to bring peace to the world, in order to benefit beings, in order to end the suffering of beings." You should cultivate that longing, really and truly. You should do that until tears are in your eyes. You will find when you begin to develop that ability those tears are not sad tears. They are the happiest tears you'll ever cry, and they are a heck of a lot more happy than going to the shopping mall and buying something new. I mean, really, that sounds like a superficial comparison, and it is. But we spend much more time at the shopping mall than we do longing to be of benefit. We should long constantly to end suffering.

You begin in that way. Then you start to think of the emptiness of self-nature, even if you don't know how to meditate. If you haven't the technique, then you might contemplate upon the emptiness of self-nature. This goes hand in hand with living the extraordinary life of compassion. They are inseparable, because along with the emptiness of self-nature is the understanding that all suffering is born of delusion. The antidote to that suffering is the annihilation of delusion. It's the same as the meditation on emptiness.

For instance, let's take a quartz crystal. It looks really, really clear. A crystal is exactly like your mind. It is exactly like the nature of your own mind in its clarity. In its natural state, it is free of any form. There is no form in there. It is said that the nature of mind is clear, self-luminous, that it exists in such a form that once any distinction is made, it is not understood. It is free of any contrivance in the same way that a crystal is free. When you look inside a crystal, you see only clarity. A better example, of course, is a crystal that is perfectly clear without any flaw, because that crystal is exactly like your mind, perfectly clear, without any flaw. You, in the natural state, are that. You are pure suchness. The moment you began to appear as you do now, was the moment you began to make distinction. In the natural state it is not so. The mind is clear, self-luminous, free of contrivance, completely relaxed. It is not gathered around itself, because it has no conceptualization of self. It's completely relaxed. It is suchness.

When you look at the crystal, you think that the crystal is like that also and it might be understood as a symbol of suchness. Now, if you were wearing a blue shirt and you put your arm behind the crystal, you would then see blue. Has the crystal become blue? Well, you have to look at it on two levels. With your arm behind it, the crystal looks blue. So, in that sense, the crystal appears to have become blue. But if you move your arm away does the crystal change? Is it still blue? So what is blue? Who perceives blue? The crystal is the same. It is the same. It is completely unaltered. What is this appearance of blue? What is this appearance of phenomena in general? This appearance of phenomena, in general, is merely conceptualization. Who is it perceived by?

Here is a very crude example, but then I told you I was born in Brooklyn. I'm not making any apologies. That's it. Let's take two objects: We have chocolate, and we have shit. Yes, shit, you heard it right! We have chocolate and we have shit. Okay, they're both brown. I'm sorry, but we have to do this. They're both brown, right? They both have a creamy consistency. So sorry! They both have a strong aroma. What makes one chocolate and the other one shit? Who determines the difference? Who is the taster? Who sees this? Who sees that? What is happening here?

All conceptualization, all phenomena arise from the belief in self-nature and from the compulsion, at that point, to make self appear separate from other, making a reactive relationship necessary. Your entire mind consists of the phenomena of hope and fear, of discrimination in a subtle and dense way. But the nature of mind itself remains steadfast, clear, uncontrived. When there is no concept of self, it is pure, perfect, it is only suchness. Only that. It cannot be altered. It remains unchanged. And the weird thing about it is, the minute that you start talking about it, you've removed yourself from the potential to understand it.

How do you get free then of distinction between shit and chocolate? How do you stop seeing the blue in the crystal? How do you perceive that true nature? Little by little, you have to disengage the idea of self, and you have to meditate on that. I recommend that you begin in this way, whether you are a dyed-in-the-wool Buddhist, or whether you are a person who has never even heard of any of this before. I don't recommend that you taste both shit and chocolate, but you can try, let's say, honey and lemon juice. Look for yourself and ask, "Who is the taster?" You say, "I taste." Then, "Where am 'I'?" Well, "I'm right here." Okay, where are you here? Let's take you apart. Let's find out where 'I' is. We'll look first in the feet. We'll start low and work up. Did you find 'I' in your feet? Take them apart. Really, you have to make slides of everything. You have to buy yourself a microscope and make slides and see if you can find 'I,' okay? Go all the way up. Look everywhere that you can, examine every single molecule. Go all the way up to the heart. Everybody thinks hearts are big these days. Let's look in the heart and see if we can find 'I.' Then we'll look in the throat. What part do you identify with the most? Do you have great legs? We'll look at your legs. Do you have a beautiful figure? We'll look at every part of it. Look at everything! Let's look in the brain. Everybody thinks they come from their head, right? So we'll look in the brain. Where is 'I'? You can even look in your eye, in your eyeball. See if you can find 'I' there.

No matter how hard you look, even if you make microscopic slides of every single part, you will not find 'I' in this body. You will not find it! Well, you say there must exist an 'I,' because how else can I go from lifetime to lifetime? And I'm telling you that the idea of 'I' is only that. It is a conceptualization that has built around it so much karmic flatulence that the profundity of it has managed to exist for lo these many eons. At that point, you can begin to understand that, essentially, nothing has happened. In truth, nothing has happened. And you can begin to meditate on the emptiness of all phenomena.

Look at a cup. Find cup in there. Take it apart. Grind it up, find cup. Cup is the idea of cup. And you can continue with everything, your house, your family. Let's take your house and examine it. Let's take your house apart. We'll put it all under the microscope. Then find family. We'll examine the people that you are calling family. Which one of them is family? We're going take them all apart, just the way we took you apart. Where are we going to find family? Family is a concept. Who made it up? You did. Where are you? I haven't found me yet!

It's crazy, but it's a good way to start practicing, because we're going to find that everything we live by—the things that make us suffer, the things that we bust our tails trying to do, everything that we do—is based upon an idea that we made up. We did! We made it up, and it has affected us for all this time. We can begin there. It's true that it would take some time to achieve realization by meditating in that way, but it's a good place to start. Meditating on the emptiness of self and phenomena can give us the foundation and the strength to live the extraordinary life of compassion that I have been talking about. It's that kind of extraordinary life of compassion, coupled with profound prayers, which will allow us to return in whatever form necessary in order to benefit beings. Even now, we will able to benefit beings if we consider this is the utmost important thing in our entire lives, and we yearn for it.

We will have a little side benefit if we do this. The side benefit is that, in the process, we will be purifying our mind of the garbage associated with self and desire we have gathered around it. We will move closer to successfully meditating on, and knowing, that profound, uncontrived, natural state of mind, just through the virtue of considering ourselves to be only important in as much as we can benefit beings, and beginning to function in that way. But, I tell you, the more we get on an ego trip about this, the more we are creating the causes of suffering and the further away we get from perceiving the natural state. Because the natural state is as it is—unpolluted, untarnished, untainted. The only thing that makes us perceive something else is that we have stuck blue in the back of the crystal, and the blue, symbolically, is conceptualization. The way to liberate the mind from the belief in the phenomena of blueness as being inherently real is to meditate on the emptiness of phenomena, the emptiness of self-nature, and to live a life that causes the purification of the mind and actually cleanses discursive thought. That is the ticket. No matter who your teacher is, if you really could talk heart to heart with any profoundly realized teacher of any religion—and I'm willing to say this publicly, any teacher, any time—if they are profoundly realized, no matter what religion they started, will tell you that the answer is the end of ego, all of its desire, and the conceptual proliferations that come with it. The realization of the natural state is the answer. That state is uncontrived, unchanging, unborn and infinite.

Whether you go the traditional Buddhist route, or whether you want to continue in a more general, yet profound route, I hope you will consider the tremendous opportunity and rewards of an extraordinary life. For you to even have the karma to come to this point where you might consider such a thing is tremendous. I urge you not waste this precious human rebirth. It's an extraordinary opportunity. You have the opportunity to see things and to hear teachings that will change your mind forever, so that in some future time, you will surely be able to benefit beings in some extraordinary way. I urge you to continue, and don't waste your time. The expression, 'don't throw your pearls before swine,' really does apply here. This is an extraordinary life, and if you were to spend it on ordinary things, it would be a shame. I hope that you will cultivate your excellent qualities and let them grow so that they will nurture all beings.

True Refuge

*If you believe that enlightenment
is the end of suffering, then that
is your object of refuge.*

In the West we have a certain context through which we understand. There's a certain karmic format that we all participate in; our thoughts are shaped a certain way. When we are children and form our ideas we all receive, individually and collectively, a certain kind of input. These things have a very important influence on us. So the way a Westerner and an Easterner might approach the Buddha's teaching is probably slightly different.

All of the cultures that practice Buddhism on a grand scale practice them from birth. The basic ideas of the Buddha's teachings permeate the entire culture. But that's not so with ours. In fact, there are some ideas that we have been brought up with that seem to be contradictory to the Buddha's teaching. From this point of view, teachings of the Buddha have to be presented in a way that we can understand that while they seem to be contradictory to what we have learned, in fact they are not.

There is a universal truth being presented that isn't contradicted by our culture, although the language and understanding is different. If something is a universal truth, then it must be true wherever it is, or it isn't true at all. So what we're looking for is a way to explain some of the basic thoughts to those that have never practiced Buddhism and haven't heard any of these teachings before.

Compassion is a foundational thought that occurs again and

again in the Buddha's teaching. But Westerners define compassion differently than Easterners, because Western ideas surrounding the concept of suffering are different than Eastern ideas. From a Westerner's point of view, we tend to think of compassion as meaning you feel sorry for somebody. It seems to be understood on a relatively superficial and ordinary level. If I say to you so and so is a compassionate person, you would think, "Oh probably he or she is kind. They probably speak nicely. They probably feed hungry people and put seed out for birds."

Now, perhaps for a people or culture more schooled in Buddhist teaching, when you say compassion or Bodhicitta, levels and levels of understanding occur within the mind simultaneously, and a more profound understanding takes place. So although as Westerners we might think it would be valuable to be compassionate, if we understood the full implications of compassion on the many different levels that it exists, we would think compassion is not only desirable, but essential. There is no life without compassion.

One of the things I would like to do is deepen our understanding of compassion so that it becomes essential. If it doesn't become essential, we have the potential at any given moment to choose to be compassionate or not. We can fall into being not compassionate. We can accidentally forget to be compassionate. All these different things can happen. You know that this is true, if you look at your life: If you remember and are mindful, you sometimes do a fairly good job. Then if you go into your natural habits, or become tired, have indigestion or PMS or whatever, you may forget and not be mindful of compassion. If we had a deeper understanding of compassion it would be part of our foundation and there would be no choice, in the same way that there's no choice about breathing. You would never think, "Well, I'm in a good mood now, I'll breathe," or, "Well breathing is okay now because I'm relaxed," or, "I can manage that now." That doesn't happen because you know that to breathe is to live. If we understood that compassion is as much a part of our being and as essential to our existence as breathing, then there would be less choice about it. It would more naturally and gracefully be part of our mind state.

In order for that to happen, we have to understand what compassion really means, and we have to understand the nature of suffering.

For Westerners, one of the basic teachings of the Buddha, that all sentient beings are suffering, is very difficult to understand. Our culture doesn't buy the idea of suffering. Most of us seem to have everything, or if we don't have everything we can get it if we really try. There are books that say if you really want to do thus and such, you can do it. That implies something about the understanding of suffering in our culture. There is also a movement that developed gradually with the idea that if you constantly think positively, you can make your life into something that is completely pleasurable all the time. This became the New Age movement.

The Buddha says that if you honestly and with courage look around, you will see that idea doesn't hold up. No matter what people's thoughts are, or how they try to live a life with positive thinking or master their emotions in that superficial way by saying, "Right now I am happy. I am constantly happy. I am always happy, therefore I will be happy"—no matter how they try to do that—we are getting old. We are getting sick. Eventually, everyone will die.

These are the thoughts we are given when we begin to study Buddhism, which turn the mind. The three sufferings of the human realm: old age, sickness and death, and also the suffering of suffering. Because even within that, there are different kinds of suffering: the suffering of loneliness, the suffering of poverty, the suffering of hunger.

We are not instructed by the Buddha to meditate on suffering to make ourselves miserable and increase our suffering. That isn't the point. The point of understanding suffering and courageously viewing suffering is that finally you will have the tools to do something about it. Because at the same time that Lord Buddha teaches us there is suffering, he also says, "And there is an end to suffering. And the end to suffering is enlightenment."

Here in the West we do everything else in order to end our suffering. We stand in front of the Estee Lauder counter for thirty years, and every year we buy a new product. We do this in order to not suffer aging; that's how we think as Westerners. We develop new and better medical techniques in order to not suffer sickness. When people die, we quickly take them off the streets and out of view and stick them in boxes. Then we claim that according to psychology one can safely grieve for nine weeks before it becomes neurosis. We have done all of these things in order to deal with old age, sickness and death. Of course we have social services and we try not to let people be too poor. If they are poor we put them all in the same part of the city so that nobody can see them. All of these things exist in our society and yet we manage to cover them up. That's really our psychology.

But if you understand a timeless and very simple truth, and look around you with courage at humans and animals all over the world, you will see suffering exists. Has Estee Lauder cured aging yet? Have we found a cure for death? Have we found a cure for sickness? We may have found a way to manipulate sickness, but it still exists. These sufferings are still there, although we have managed to delude ourselves that they don't exist. The problem is that it's not the cure. The cure is realization, enlightenment.

In order to accomplish the end of all suffering, we as a culture have to turn some of our attention away from the grand cover up, and more to the pursuit of the real cure. We have to finally understand our objects of refuge.

Now, I'm a red-blooded American. You can't get any more American than born in Brooklyn to an Italian father and a Jewish mother. That's as American as they come in this world. So I understand our culture. I don't claim to have any special powers or abilities; in fact I could study Lord Buddha's teachings for the next twenty thousand lives. It's the same for everyone: until you reach supreme enlightenment, you don't understand the Buddha's teaching, because to do that you must understand the Buddha's mind. I feel that I am a beginner. But one thing I do understand is that as Westerners we have not yet come to understand what our objects of refuge are. One of our main sufferings, and the cause of more suffering, is that we take refuge in the wrong things.

As a culture we have not come to understand the value of using this life as a vehicle to achieve supreme realization. Even for those of us practicing Dharma, it takes a long time to understand that the only value of this precious human rebirth is to achieve enlightenment. Here in America we have the most precious jewel of all: the leisure to practice. If we don't have the time, we can make the time. You can. Try it. You can. We have the leisure to practice. We have the ability to study. We have within our grasp a true path that has proven again and again and again it can produce enlightenment. We have these precious things, and yet we don't understand that the only point of this life is to end suffering, not only for ourselves but for all sentient beings. Because once we ourselves achieve realization, we can contribute to the end of suffering in a real way for all sentient beings. For all others.

We tend to think of our lives in a very different way, because we don't understand what our objects of refuge are. We try to live our lives with immediate gratification. We think, "Well, I have to be busy because I have to have this and this and this and this and this and this. I have to buy this, and I have to have this and I have to attain this." We don't accept that maybe it is possible to live a completely successful life under a completely different set of rules.

The idea of renunciation is not popular in our country because we don't understand it. In America we believe in accumulation. That's our source of refuge: We accumulate. The minute we have that coffee pot and that microwave and that big-screen TV and all those different things, we're going to be happy. If you don't have a car, if you're not rich, if you don't have a toaster, if you don't have a dishwasher, if you don't have all of these things, that is the cause of suffering. Yet the Buddha says, 'No, that's not the case. The cause of suffering is the desire for those things.' Having devoted ourselves to accumulation, it becomes uncomfortable to think that we might have to dedicate our lives to renunciation.

It depends on your objects of refuge. If you really think that the coffee percolator, the TV, the anti-aging cream, the microwave, the big car and all the money are your source of refuge, then most Americans are practicing their religion correctly. But if you believe that enlightenment is the end of suffering, then that is your object of refuge. All the teachings and the supports to the Path to enlightenment—the Buddha, the Dharma or the Buddha's teaching, and the Sangha or the Buddha's community—are the objects of refuge. That is what you see as the solution. The things like toaster can only make toast. The things like coffee pot can only make coffee. The things like TV can only show whatever they show. They are not sources of refuge; they never, ever, end suffering for more than a short period of time. If we understand that our true sources of refuge are those things which end suffering, we'll be able to perceive in a logical and real way.

We are a hard-working people. We get up very early in the morning. We quickly get ready under stressful conditions, putting on as much of those Estee Lauder things as we possibly can, before seven o'clock. Then we leave and stay on the road for a very long time, under terrible conditions. Then we get somewhere and we work very hard with people we don't know very well, doing very strange things that are very different from our nature, all day long. Then we come home on a very long road that is also very difficult to travel. Then we eat very quickly, and don't feel very well, watch TV and go to bed. That's what most of our culture does. And it's a very hard road.

We use so much energy doing things that we are told we must do. We must have a certain level of education. We must have a certain level of accumulation. We must care for these things that we have accumulated. We must cultivate certain kinds of relationships. That's a big job. According to our culture there are certain lines that we have to cross in order to be successful and happy. We work very hard at these things.

But chronically and repeatedly at certain ages of our lives we go through phases or passages when we are dissatisfied. Marriages go through the seven-year itch. We go through middle age and we go through menopause. We go through all these different stages, and they're so common and usual that our psychologists are beginning to recognize and document them and consider some of them normal.

What are they really? We work very hard to get to a certain phase of our life and then we find that it's basically empty. We didn't get the satisfaction we were promised. Then we gear ourselves up for another phase. When we get there, suddenly we find: uh oh. That's not to say we don't have our little joys and happinesses along the way. But basically as a people we work very hard and yet are becoming deeply disappointed and disillusioned.

The way that some of us have chosen to deal with it is to think more positively and convince ourselves that we really are happy. We go to friends or support groups or some New Age groups or a psychologist, all the different avenues that people explore when they're really hurting. What you basically come out with is, "Oh you have to change your thinking around." You are told to think, "My life is full, my life is fruitful, I am really happy and I like being busy like this because it means that I'm having many experiences." There are so many people doing that kind of thing it's painful to watch. Some people are okay with that; it's their karma to live a good and simple life, and throughout their life they try to be kind to others. But some people are really struggling.

I wish from my heart that it would be okay to be a renunciate. Because to be a renunciate is to renounce the things that one has desire for, the objects that one grasps, and instead seek only a true source of refuge. To renounce the sources of suffering: There ought to be a place for that in our society. It ought to be okay for anyone to do what they want. It ought to be okay if they want to remain as they are and continue to function in the ordinary ways that we are used to in our society. But it ought to be okay if a person sincerely becomes discontented and wants to seek a supreme refuge that is the end of suffering, which is enlightenment.

You don't necessarily have to be a Buddhist to adopt these kinds of ideas, although I found for myself that the Buddha's teaching was the best way to do it. But not only Buddhists can do this kind of thing. In order to do this successfully you have to determine what your supreme refuge is. You have to really review that. This is why I like what the Buddha said, because in the foundational teachings you are never asked to buy something with blind faith. You're asked to think things out logically.

This is what I suggest you should do. Think to yourself, "Really, how do people suffer? How do sentient beings suffer?" Sentient beings of all kinds, not only people. If you can learn anything about non-physical sentient beings, do that. The Buddha has many teachings on non-physical realms. But, even about just the ones that you know, human beings and animals. Check books out from the library on different life forms and different conditions around the world. Check out books about India. Check out books about Ethiopia. Check out books about different cultures and different ways in which people live. Check out books about different animals and different life forms. How they grow, how they evolve, from insects to lions. Study them all carefully.

You will see that animals are consumed: that they are eaten, and that they eat. That human beings grow sick, grow old, and that they die. That so far, no one has definitely proven they can keep from doing that. Even within that, there are sub-sufferings and different kinds of sufferings. While you are studying all of those things, develop a deep sense of compassion for the endlessness of it—compassion for the lack of resolution and that everything around you will have its moment of intense suffering, everything and everyone. Develop a deep sense of compassion, that their suffering is endless. That it is unbearable at times. And that there is yet no solution. Think for yourself: What could be the possible solution? Try to think one up. Really work that through, down to the place where you're into the planning stages. You will find it will never work, because we are all filled with the karma of desire. Every one of us.

Having decided for yourself that all sentient beings are suffering so greatly that you can no longer bear it, and having understood that there is nothing else but to end this suffering, then maybe you might also think there's no other way to spend your life other than to accomplish that for yourself and other sentient beings. Because the only way you can truly benefit beings is if you yourself have achieved some realization and understanding of the causes of their suffering.

Having understood all these things, then you must determine for yourself how you will spend the rest of your life. You must determine this, and it will take every day of your life, because we've been trained to do the opposite. You must think for yourself again and again and again: Of what use is this life? If I am constantly filled with more suffering, if I am constantly participating in a scenario that always ends up with suffering, how will this life be of any value? And if you come to the solution that this life has value if it is a vehicle for enlightenment, then you should think for yourself, how should I do this? You should examine what you do now; how you spend your day. Then you should think, how have I spent my years? Then you should think, what should I do?

One of the problems that we Westerners have is that we've grown up with religions that say God is external. That is not what the Buddha teaches. The Buddha teaches us not that our supreme object of refuge is an external God, but that ultimately, in the deepest sense, our supreme refuge is enlightenment, the uncontrived natural state free of desire. According to the Buddha's teaching, it is possible to achieve realization, that desire-free state; and the natural uncontrived wisdom state is attainable. According to which path you take, it is attainable in many lifetimes, it is attainable in some lifetimes, it is attainable in a few lifetimes, or according to the Vajrayana, with sincere practice it is attainable in one lifetime.

You have to decide for yourself what you're going to do. It's a difficult job, because we are so filled with ideas from our up-bringing. People say, "I'm moved by what you say, but I just don't know if I can renounce everything. I just don't know if I can give everything up." That's not what's being talked about here. What's being talked about is that you have to determine your objects of refuge. You have to determine what your ref-uge is, and from that you should make your own decisions. There are many different levels at which you can practice. You can become a full renunciate, taking vows, taking robes. You can also practice in a more casual way, laying the pathway for eventual deeper practice. Nobody's making a rule for you. The point is that you should think for yourself and you should think past the ways in which you were brought up. You should look courageously at suffering, at the causes for suffering, and at the end of suffering.

According to the Buddha's teaching, there is nothing on this Earth that can end suffering for all sentient beings. If we found the cure for cancer, AIDS, for everything, something else would happen, because the karma of sickness is there. If we found the cure for poverty, something else would happen. If we found the cure for war.... and all these ifs are mighty big. The karma of suffering is desire. It is the root cause for all suffering. Having determined that, we have to think that to get rid of it from our mindstreams will take something more profound than manipu-lating our external environment. The problem cannot be solved in that way.

I think it behooves us as Westerners to think deeply about these things. From my point of view, I have seen Westerners adapt the Buddhist religion, and I am not satisfied in the way that they are doing it. They're practicing Buddhists, they know the mudras, they know the mantras, and they know how to ring the bells. They know how to do all the ceremonial things that come with the Buddhadharma; and I am not happy with their minds. Because maybe they didn't take long enough to decide for themselves what the object of refuge is and what the cause of suffering is.

You can collect Dharma in a materialistic way just as well as you can collect cars and TVs. You can collect Lamas and the blessings of Lamas in a materialistic way just as easily as you can do anything else. You can collect new thoughts and new ideas and spiritual truths and books and all kinds of things, and never change. Or you can come from a really pure place and examine these things with courage and with pure intention. You can be determined to awaken the seed and the fire of compassion in your mind by examining the suffering of all sentient beings. You can encourage that flame, that fire, fanning it into life so that it burns away all obstacles to your practice. And you'll find for yourself your object of refuge, and you'll go...just go. You can do that. It takes courage and it takes pure intention and it takes determination to really think about these things, in a logical and real way. That's what I hope you will do.

I am a Buddhist, and I always will be. But I'm not trying to sell Buddhism. What I would like to see is a world without suffering. That is the point, hopefully, of all religions; certainly of mine. I wish to talk about the same thing Lord Buddha himself talked about: the causes of suffering and the end of suffering. If we start there, thinking of these things and thinking of them with what Buddhists call fervent regard, we can make a lot of progress.

Contemplating these things creates a great deal of virtue and merit. After you think about these things, please dedicate the time that you spent and the effort that you took, to benefit all sentient beings (see Dedication Prayer, page 105). In other words, offer the virtue or the merit that you have accomplished by even just wanting to love. There's a tremendous amount of virtue in that. Offer that as food and drink to all sentient beings so that the karma of that can be shared with a world that is suffering.

Bodhicitta
The Practice of Loving

*Compassion and enlightenment
can never be separated.*

Compassion is a subject that should be of interest to everyone. There isn't one person that should consider themselves exempt from the practice of loving. We know from our own lives, I'm sure, that the times we have been the happiest are the times that we have loved. And the times that we have been the most useful are the times that we have been loving.

Compassion is one of the foundational teachings of Mahayana Buddhism, but it is more extensive than the kind of loving we find in our lives. From the Mahayana view, we should seek to love all sentient beings equally. It is a very interesting point of view, because you would think it more natural to love your husband or your wife, your parents and your children, more than you would love others. Buddhists are taught to honor our parents and to maintain the integrity of family, to not have divorces and go from family to family. Yet the Buddhist perspective is that all sentient beings are essentially equal, that their needs are equal and that all sentient beings equally desire happiness. It is useful and beneficial to love everyone and to experience compassion for all beings equally.

We are taught the very reason we love certain people more than others is because in our minds we have the karma of attachment and aversion. We have hope and fear within our minds, and these things are based on the belief in our own ego structure, the belief that self-nature is inherently real. Our relationships with others are shadowed by that and take on the flavor of whatever particular energy suits our particular ego. Because of our ego, we think that we love one person more than we love another.

If we existed somehow miraculously in an egoless state, we would find that all sentient beings are equal and have the same nature. They are that same primordial, natural suchness. Seeing each sentient being as that would help us understand that there is essentially no difference. We are all exactly the same, we all desire happiness and haven't yet developed the skills to get that happiness. We are all deserving of love and caring and nurturing and being taught the skills of happiness.

What is it about compassion that is so important? Why do you hear so much about it in the Buddha's teaching? From the Mahayana point of view there are two different kinds of compassion, or Bodhicitta. Bodhicitta actually means mind of enlightenment. The mind of compassion—the fully functional, fully awakened mind of compassion—is the same, and not different from, the mind of enlightenment. You cannot achieve enlightenment without developing the mind of compassion. You cannot achieve compassion—true compassion, selfless compassion—without moving ever closer to the mind of enlightenment. Essentially they are the same.

In our language we have two different words for fully awakened compassion and enlightenment, but from the Buddhist perspective when you say Bodhicitta you mean compassion and you also mean enlightenment. Due to the structure of our language, we actually separate the two. Yet they cannot be separated. Compassion and enlightenment can never be separated.

It's impossible. The reason why we seek to express the mind of compassion, and why we emphasize it, is to accomplish our own purpose and the purpose of others. We want to achieve enlightenment.

According to the Buddha's teaching all sentient beings have experienced suffering and continue to suffer. We have old age, sickness and death. We don't know what to do about them. We get run over by cars and all kinds of crazy things happen to us on a regular basis. The Buddha teaches us the only way to end suffering is to achieve enlightenment. Once we achieve enlightenment, the very root causes that produce suffering, the seeds of karma within our mind, are eradicated.

We want to achieve enlightenment in order to attain happiness for all beings. That is the reason we enter the spiritual path and really pursue it in a determined fashion. If we were to look past the level of our mind that is constantly developing new and wonderful concepts, we would find that there is a basic primordial natural state. That natural state, free of conceptualization, that suchness, is the very fabric that is the mother of all phenomena, including your own self. The natural primordial nature that cannot be described is your nature and it is everyone's nature and it is the same nature; there is no point at which you can divide it. When you divide it you start believing in self-nature or the ego structure. At that point, you are not experiencing the primordial state any longer.

The truth of the matter is there is only that natural state. It is free of conceptualization, it is self-luminous, it is all-embracing, it is pure, and it remains and will always be undefiled. That is the natural state. If we are all one in that way—if that is what truly exists—then it is not possible for us to be separate. The Bodhisattva's or the Buddha's point of view is that I cannot achieve enlightenment without you. I cannot. Because that which I truly am is the same as you. If I separate myself from you, I've missed the point somehow. It is as important for all sentient beings to achieve enlightenment and to be free of suffering as it is for me and for you, individually, to accomplish that.

Thus the idea of compassion becomes more than an idea. It becomes the basis or the foundation of enlightenment. It becomes the only thing with meaning. That being the case, we must think about the ways in which compassion or Bodhicitta are practiced. There are two levels of Bodhicitta. There is aspirational Bodhicitta or aspirational compassion, and there is practical compassion.

Aspirational Bodhicitta is just as it sounds. It is the aspiring to compassion, or the wishing for compassionate activity. You should not think that because it is only wishing it is not precious and valuable. It is absolutely precious and valuable because it is the kind of contemplation that provides the basis or foundation on which you build your ability to practice practical compassion.

In the Vajrayana tradition one contemplates very deeply on certain thoughts before you ever go on to any deeper practice, and these thoughts are called the 'Four Thoughts that Turn the Mind.' The idea is that your mind becomes turned in such a way that your intention to practice is firm, like a rock. If you were wishy-washy about why you should practice meditation, your meditation will be wishy-washy. There's no doubt about it. If you were convinced that your job could bring you more eternal and natural happiness than enlightenment, you would practice your job with greater fervor than you would practice enlightenment. Therefore you try to turn your mind so that it has a firm foundation, hard as a rock, upon which you can build your practice.

It's that way with aspirational Bodhicitta. You have to turn your mind in such a way that you understand the value of compassion and you have to actually ignite your mind. You have to set it on fire, and that fire has to be stronger and hotter and fiercer than any other feeling or idea that you have. It has to burn so strongly that you can't put it out.

In order to practice aspirational Bodhicitta, you must first of all look around you with courage. Because we Americans, even New Age Americans, don't like to look around and see that others are suffering. We hate to think about that. We think somehow it's bad to think like that. According to the Buddha, it isn't bad to think like that. In fact, you must think like that in order to go on to the next level of practice. You must look around you and be honest and be courageous. If you don't see suffering in your life, if you don't know that the people around you are lonely or getting old or getting sick, that they live with worry and with fear, then what you need to do is go to the library and check out books about other cultures and other forms of life, and see what the rest of the world is like. Have you ever seen pictures of Calcutta, India? Have you ever seen pictures of Bangladesh? Have you ever seen pictures of Africa? If you don't believe that suffering exists in the world, you'll see it there. Have you ever studied the lives of people who continually do non-virtuous activity? Even though they might look like they're tough and in control, they are deeply suffering. It behooves you to be courageous enough to examine that. You should look at other life forms. You should look at animals. You should look and see how oxen are treated in India. I speak of India a lot, not because it's a bad place, but because I've been there, and I was shocked. I had no idea how sheltered Americans are from suffering. I had no idea until I saw lepers in the street with no limbs and with open sores.

Having studied these things, you will come to understand that there is suffering in the world. You should cultivate in your heart and mind a feeling of great compassion. You shouldn't stop until you've come to the point that you are on fire and you cannot bear that they are suffering so much. The Buddha says that we have had so many incarnations in so many different forms that every being you see, every one, has been your mother or your father. Whether you believe that or not, it's a great way to think. Because you look at other beings and see how they are suffering helplessly, with no way to get out of it. And that they, at one time, have given you birth. In that way, you can come to love them in a way that you can practice for them.

You should allow yourself to become so filled with the urgency to practice loving that your heart is on fire and there's no other subject that interests you as much, even if it's uncomfortable. We Americans think we should never be uncomfortable. Sometimes discomfort is very useful. Be uncomfortable and let yourself ache with the need to practice Bodhicitta. Cultivate in yourself that urgency and that determination. You might get to the point where you feel something, and you feel sort of sorry for all sentient beings. You might think, "Okay, now I've got it. I'll go on to the next step." No, you haven't got it. You should cultivate compassion from this moment until you reach supreme enlightenment.

Unless they are supremely enlightened no one is born with the perfect mind of compassion. I, and everyone I teach and everyone I know, including my teachers, practice aspirational Bodhicitta everyday, reminding ourselves that all sentient beings suffer unbearably and that we find it unbearable to see. You should continue to cultivate compassion every moment of your life. It will begin to burn in your heart. It's like love. It's beautiful. You won't want ever to be without that divine fire in your heart. It will warm you as no other love can. It will stabilize your mind as no other practice can.

Having understood that all sentient beings are suffering, and having cultivated in your mind the aspiration of Bodhicitta, you should make fervent wishing prayers, constant wishing prayers. My teachers have told me that time and again great Bodhisattvas have been born in India and Tibet and their practice was not that extensive. They were not very educated in their practice; they were very simple people. But they were known in their previous incarnation for the heart-felt wishing prayers that they made. Because of the depth to which they desired to benefit beings, and through the force of their prayers alone, they were reborn in a form in which they could benefit a great many beings. So those prayers are exquisite.

Wishing prayers are important. They should be done in the morning and they should be done in the evening. They should be done every moment that you can be mindful of them. Make fervent prayers in your mind and your heart that you will, in this lifetime, benefit many beings and end their suffering. And that in all future lifetimes you will be reborn in a form in which you can benefit beings so that they might achieve enlightenment and have their suffering ended. Make prayers to cultivate in yourself that mind of enlightenment and to cultivate in yourself the pure intention to achieve enlightenment in order to benefit beings. That is the aspirational Bodhicitta, or practice of compassion.

All of our suffering is brought about because we have desire in our mindstreams. Having desire, we have attachment and aversion, hope and fear. Examine your own thoughts. Every one of them is either a thought of hope or a thought of fear. There isn't one that doesn't have as an underlying cause, hope or fear, attraction or aversion. Every one. That is the way the mind of duality works. So all of the experiences that we have, according to the Buddha, are caused by the karma of desire. Making wishing prayers to return in a form in which you can benefit beings purifies the mind of desire. You will find that desire rules your mind less and less. Compassion is the great stabilizer of the mind.

Never stop cultivating aspirational Bodhicitta. While you are practicing aspirational Bodhicitta, your mind becomes firm and stabilized. You are so on fire that you need to practice, in the same way that because you are determined to live, you always remember to breathe. With that intensity, you should be absolutely determined to accomplish compassion and benefit all beings. You always remember to practice and be mindful. Then you begin to practice practical Bodhicitta.

Practical Bodhicitta has two divisions. It has a lesser and greater division, or personal and a transpersonal division. Compassion on the personal level is what we call ordinary human kindness.

It is invaluable. There is never a time in your life that you should not practice ordinary human kindness. I am sometimes dismayed at people who have a high-fallutin' idea about compassion and how to practice the Vajrayana path, and they know how to do the proper instrumentation and they can chant and they can do all these wonderful things. But they aren't kind to one another. How you can think of yourself as a real practitioner and not even be nice to the person next to you? How can you be arrogant?

Ordinary human kindness must be constantly practiced. If you know of someone who is hungry, you should do your best to feed them. If a starving child were in front of you, wouldn't you feed him or her? If someone that you loved really was lonely, wouldn't you try to help them? Of course, these are ordinary human kindnesses. We're not even perfect in that, are we? I mean, we let ourselves and our families down. We let everybody down on a regular basis. Sometimes ordinary human kindness is impossible to achieve.

Ordinary human kindness is not lesser in its fabric or nature, but it touches less people. For instance, let's say you needed a friend. If I were to stay with you for some period of time, we would talk and we would share. Maybe I would teach you to meditate, if I were to discover that you're the kind of person that would really respond to that. But if I don't do that, maybe I'll have the time to teach a large group of people. Essentially I might be able to benefit many people as opposed to benefiting one person, even though you are very important and precious to me. Yet even teaching a larger group of people is actually an intermediate level of practice. There are only so many people that can fit in this room and can be taught.

What is the highest level of compassion? What is the highest level of Bodhicitta? You have to go back to the Buddha's teaching to figure this one out. The Buddha says that all sentient beings are suffering and that there is an end to suffering and that the end to suffering is enlightenment. That's the only true end to suffering. If you fed every one that's hungry everyday and provided them each with a companion so that they're never lonely, gave them nice clothes, they still will experience old age, sickness and death. There's nothing you can do about that. And you have no control over how they will be reborn in their next incarnation. They could come back in a form in which they still suffer. The only end to suffering is to eradicate the cause of suffering from the mindstream.

The root cause of all suffering is the belief in self-nature as being inherently real. It's the mother of all-pervasive desire in the mindstream. The children are hatred, greed and ignorance. The mind of duality causes us to act in certain ways that create the karma so that our lives manifest in certain ways. If we suffer from hunger or old age or sickness or death, whatever it is that we suffer from, the root cause for those sufferings is the belief that self-nature is inherently real. How can you possibly uproot all of that from your mindstream? How can you rid the very seed of suffering from your mindstream? According to the Buddha, that is to achieve enlightenment. To help sentient beings remove these causes from their mindstreams, we must ourselves first achieve enlightenment. The purpose of self, which is to achieve enlightenment, is the same as the purpose of other, which is to achieve enlightenment. They are the same. In the same way that we are non-dual, these purposes are non-dual.

While striving to accomplish the mind of compassion in such a way that we can benefit beings, we must also, at the same time, and with the same determination for the sake of sentient beings, strive to achieve enlightenment for ourselves. We must do it for their sake. Enlightenment cannot be accomplished for any selfish reason. Having seen the suffering of others you might be able to bring about the fire of compassion; you have that potential. And for that reason, you can practice.

According to the Buddha's teaching only a fully enlightened being can bring about the end of suffering through offering teachings that bring about enlightenment. Therefore as you strive to be compassionate to sentient beings, and practice both aspirational and practical Bodhicitta, at the same time, and with the same energy and fervent regard, you should strive to achieve enlightenment for their sake. The moment that you forget that you are doing this for their sake, you will not have the fire that you cultivated so carefully to push you along.

From the Mahayana point of view, the purpose of self and of others is the same and cannot be separated. We strive to achieve enlightenment, yet when we come to the very brink of enlightenment we hang back, so that we can reincarnate again and again in cyclic existence, solely to benefit beings. So that we can take an emanation form in cyclic existence in order to bring about the end of suffering. There are some beautiful Mahayana prayers, and you don't have to be a Buddhist to love them.

Where there is hunger, let me appear as food.
Where there is a deep river, let me appear as a bridge.
Where there is sorrow, let me appear as the comforter.
Where there is war, let me appear as a peacemaker.

Having no thought for yourself, you should pray endlessly that you can bring about the end of suffering of others in whatever way is needed. I promise you, if you make those prayers in a heartfelt way, your mind will be purified to such an extent that you will achieve your goal. You will be born in a form in which you can benefit beings.

You do not have to be a Buddhist to think in the way that I have just described. Compassion belongs to no religion. The mind of enlightenment is inherently your mind; it is the natural state in which you exist. But it becomes occluded and poisoned and tainted by desire, and by hatred, greed and ignorance. The mother of it all is the belief that self-nature is inherently real. Why is that the mother? Because once you believe in self-nature or the ego as being inherently real, everything you think, everything you feel, everything you decide must support that ego. It will try to survive. But by practicing in this deeply and profoundly compassionate way, that karma begins to dilute. The desire, and the hatred, greed and ignorance that come from the belief in self-nature as being inherently real begin to subside. The mind relaxes and it becomes clearer and more capable of understanding, even if just for a moment, its natural state in meditation.

Only through the practice of aspirational and practical compassion can one achieve enlightenment. It will take some time, and it will take fervent practice. But you should think that this is a good place to start. The only vow you have to take is the one you have always wanted to take. A Vow of Love.

DEDICATION

By this effort may all sentient beings be free of suffering.

May their minds be filled with the nectar of virtue.

In this way may all causes resulting in suffering be extinguished,

And only the light of compassion shine throughout all realms.

— Jetsunma Ahkön Norbu Lhamo

To read more of Jetsunma's teachings visit her blog.

Tibetan Buddhist Altar ❖ www.tibetanbuddhistaltar.org

GLOSSARY

Aspirational Bodhicitta: The wish to attain the greatest good for the sake of all beings by engaging in the necessary steps to achieve Buddhahood.

Awake/Awakened: A term used interchangeably for enlightenment. (See also 'Buddha' and 'Enlightened' in this Glossary.)

Bodhicitta: The mind of enlightenment that encompasses wisdom and compassion.

Bodhisattva: One who embodies Bodhicitta. A Bodhisattva vows to rescue all beings from their suffering and guide them to enlightenment.

Buddha: The historical founder of Buddhism, Shakyamuni. Also, one who is completely awake to his or her true nature and the true nature of all reality.

Buddhadharma: The Buddhist teachings and practices.

Buddhist: One who, from the depths of their heart, has taken refuge in the Three Precious Jewels of Buddhism—the Buddha, Dharma, and Sangha. (See also 'Refuge' in this Glossary.)

Compassion: Activity motivated by concern for others. (See also Practical Compassion/Bodhicitta and Aspirational Compassion/Bodhicitta in this Glossary.)

Conceptualization: Perception, thoughts and reason are all concepts in our mind to identify objects perceived physically or mentally as separate from oneself. (See also 'Self-nature' and 'Phenomena' in this Glossary.)

Cyclic Existence: The cycle of death and rebirth in the six realms in which one is endlessly propelled according to causes and results. (See also 'Karma' in this Glossary.) The six realms are God, Demi-god, Human, Animal, Hungry Ghost and Hell realms.

Deity: Aspects of the Buddha: the great richness of enlightened mind expressing itself in countless forms of energy and light, including meditational deities manifesting in a variety of forms displaying enlightened qualities.

Dharma: The pure path taught by the Buddha that leads one out of suffering into the awakened state of enlightenment. Dharma is the underlying meaning of the Buddha's teachings; the truth upon which all Buddhist practices, scriptures, and philosophy are based.

Dzogchen: The pith teachings of the Nyingma school of Tibetan Buddhism otherwise known as the "Great Perfection." The Dzogchen teachings have been passed down in an unbroken line from teacher to student from the Primordial Buddha Samantabhadra to the present day, retaining all their freshness, immediacy and power. Dzogchen is the highest teachings of the Nyingma school of Tibetan Buddhism.

Emptiness: The complete absence of inherent existence in all phenomena.

Enlightenment: Enlightenment is the cessation of suffering, reached when the qualities of compassion and wisdom are perfected, and all non-virtue has been extinguished from one's mind.

Ignorance: One of the main causes of suffering along with hatred and greed; a lack of awareness of cause and effect relationships.

Incarnation: The form one takes lifetime after lifetime in any one of the six realms. (See also 'Cyclic Existence' in this Glossary.)

Kali Yuga: An extended and cyclical age of world degeneration in Buddhist Cosmology that includes the current time period.

Karma: Universal law of cause and effect governing the activity of unenlightened beings, whereby all experience is the result or fruit of some previous action or cause. Through the force of intention we perform actions with our body, speech, and mind, and all of these actions produce effects. The effect of virtuous actions is happiness and the effect of non-virtuous actions is suffering.

Mahayana: One of the three vehicles or streams of Buddhism—the other two being Theravada and Vajrayana. The cultivation of Bodhicitta is central to the practice of Mahayana Buddhism.

Meditation: Encompasses various forms of mind practice to increase spiritual awareness. There are two principal forms of meditation practice: the development of concentration and the development of insight.

Mindstream: The apparent continuum of ordinary consciousness created by karmic imprints which carry over from lifetime to lifetime.

Obscurations: Factors, e.g., hatred, greed, ignorance, that conceal one's Buddha nature preventing the attainment of Enlightenment.

Phenomena: The objects of direct experience as perceived by 'self'.

Practical Compassion/Bodhicitta: Practices necessary for achieving the goal of Enlightenment, e.g., love, compassion, generosity.

Practice: Any activity that moves one closer to the goal of Enlightenment. This can include meditation, contemplation, mantra recitation, and prayer.

Primordial: The fundamental, natural state; the ground of being.

Refuge: In the Buddhist context, the objects that protect us from suffering, e.g., the Buddha, the Buddha's teachings and the community of practitioners.

Self-nature: Ego structure.

Sentient Being: A sentient being is any living being that experiences feelings through their senses, and also refers to a being who has not yet reached enlightenment.

Suchness: The fundamental, natural state. (See also 'Primordial' in this Glossary.)

Vajrayana: One of the three vehicles of Buddhism that also contains the other vehicles—Theravada and Mahayana—within it. Vajrayana, otherwise known as the "Diamond Vehicle," is practiced mostly by Buddhists following the Tibetan, Mongolian and Himalayan forms of Buddhism.

About Jetsunma Ahkön Norbu Lhamo

From an early age, Jetsunma Ahkön Norbu Lhamo has devoted herself to meditation and the alleviation of suffering in the world. With confirmation from two highly revered Tibetan Buddhist masters, His Holiness Dilgo Khyentse Rinpoche and Dzongnang Rinpoche, His Holiness Penor Rinpoche, 11th throneholder of the Palyul Lineage in the Nyingma tradition, recognized Jetsunma as a reincarnation of the 17th century yogini Genyenma Ahkön Lhamo.  The first Ahkön Lhamo was the sister of Rigdzin Kunzang Sherab, the founder and first Throneholder of Palyul.

Subsequently, His Holiness Kusum Lingpa recognized Jetsunma as an emanation of Princess Lhacham Mandarava, the Indian consort of Padmasambhava (also known as Guru Rinpoche, or Precious Teacher), the Indian scholar who stabilized Buddhism in Tibet. Jetsunma is the first Western woman to have been officially recognized and enthroned as a Tulku, an enlightened being who reincarnates in whatever form necessary to benefit sentient beings.

With innate compassion and wisdom, and drawing on her experiences as a Western woman, Jetsunma makes even the most profound Buddhist teachings accessible. Her teachings, often infused with humor, reach a broad audience, including long-time Buddhist practitioners as well as people simply wanting to live with kindness and generosity. Jetsunma encourages each of us to create a world of compassion, by contemplating the suffering of others, and taking action to bring about change.

CPSIA information can be obtained
at www.ICGtesting.com
Printed in the USA
LVHW02s0811070318
568944LV00020B/94/P